# Making History

# The Age of Invasions

## Britain 55 BC–AD 1200

## John Patrick

Formerly Lecturer in History
Aberdeen College of Education

## Mollie Packham

Formerly Head of History
Falmer School, Brighton

Illustrations by Susan Bird

John Murray

# Acknowledgements

Mollie Packham is grateful to the following for their help and advice: David Burrell, School of Education, Sussex University; John Fines, West Sussex Institute of Higher Education; Miss Maisie Carter, Education Library, Sussex University; and Miss G. E. Carruthers, Shoreham Public Library, West Sussex.

The authors and publishers would like to thank Dr Martin Booth of Cambridge University Department of Education for his help in the preparation of this series.

Thanks are due to the following for permission to reproduce copyright photographs:
p. 2, reproduced by permission of The National Museum of Wales; p. 8, The Grosvenor Museum, Chester; pp. 9, 11, 92, 121 (top), reproduced by permission of the controller, HMSO; p. 13, British Tourist Authority; pp. 14, 19 (bottom), 44, 45, 47, 96, 98, 101, 122, John Patrick; pp. 17, 21 (bottom left), 22 (bottom), Museum of London; pp. 21 (top), 39 (right), 75, The Ashmolean Museum; pp. 21 (bottom right), 22 (top), 39 (left), 48, The British Museum; pp. 30 (right), 32 (left), 37 (left), 51 (bottom), 73, 104 (top), 109, 114, 115, 118 (bottom), 127, The British Library; p. 32 (left), Biblioteca Medicea Laurenziana, Florence; pp. 32 (right), 94 (bottom), 109 (right), 117, National Monuments Record; pp. 37 (right), 53, The Bodleian Library; p. 38, Alan Sorrell; p. 41 (left), Trinity College Library, Cambridge; pp. 58, 61, 64, Nationalmuseet, Copenhagen; pp. 62 (left), 69, University Museum of National Antiquities, Oslo; p. 66, The Manx Museum; p. 67 (right), National Museum of Iceland; p. 67 (left), Statens Historiska Museum, Stockholm; p. 77, Crown copyright; pp. 83, 84, 86, 99 (top), 104 (bottom), 105 (top), The Phaidon Picture Archive; p. 93 (top), B. T. Batsford Ltd; p. 99 (bottom), The Public Record Office; p. 101 (bottom), reproduced by permission of the Scottish Development Department; p. 103, Archives de la Seine-maritime; p. 105 (bottom), Ronald Sheridan's Photo-Library; pp. 119, 124, The Dean and Chapter of Durham; p. 121 (top), The Welsh Office; pp. 134, 137, 139, Professor Leslie Alcock, Glasgow University.

The following have been adapted from the sources listed:
p. 10, Shepherd's *Historical Atlas*; p. 12, survey by A. C. Dickie and R. C. Bosanquet; pp. 20, 22, P. Marsden, *Roman London*; p. 25, R. W. Ford; p. 27, K. Branigan; p. 41, Andrea Pinnington; p. 43, Penguin, *History of Britain* Volume 2; p. 107, J. Hutchins, *Dorset* (1761); p. 118, The Historical Association.

© Mollie Packham and John Patrick 1985

First published 1985
by John Murray (Publishers) Ltd
50 Albemarle Street, London W1X 4BD

Reprinted (revised) 1986, 1989

Typeset by Fakenham Photosetting Ltd
Printed and bound in Great Britain
at The Bath Press, Avon

British Library Cataloguing in Publication Data
Patrick, John
    The age of invasions.—(making history)
    1. Great Britain—History—to 1485
    I. Title  II. Packham, Mollie  III. Series
    942        DA130

    ISBN 0–7195–4122–0

£6·85

# Making History
# The Age of Invasions

# Making History

# Contents

# Introduction

The *Making History* series does not set out to provide a continuous narrative covering the whole of British history. Instead it aims to study the history of Britain in the context of the wider world. It emphasises both the links which, throughout its history, have bound Britain to other countries, and the multicultural heritage of the British people.

Each of the first three books in the series has five main units linked by a broad common theme. Each unit explores selected aspects of British life during a particular period, bringing it to life in a way that would be impossible in a general survey.

Book 1, *The Age of Invasions*, studies British history during the period when the country was invaded and taken over by successive waves of foreigners—Romans, Anglo-Saxons, Vikings and lastly Normans and Plantagenets. Each unit begins by focusing on a particular individual. In addition, the section *Roads to Camelot* presents an inquiry based on the Arthurian legends in which pupils are provided with evidence about the period and encouraged to evaluate it and come to their own conclusions.

Each book contains a wide range of graded, skills-based follow-up exercises and activities which are centred on the text but also expand the themes and ideas contained in the text and introduce new material. Each book also contains a section on topic work. This encourages pupils to follow up some of the themes running through the book in more detail and offers guidance on how to find and present material.

**Note**
Words printed in **bold type** are explained on pages 144 and 145.

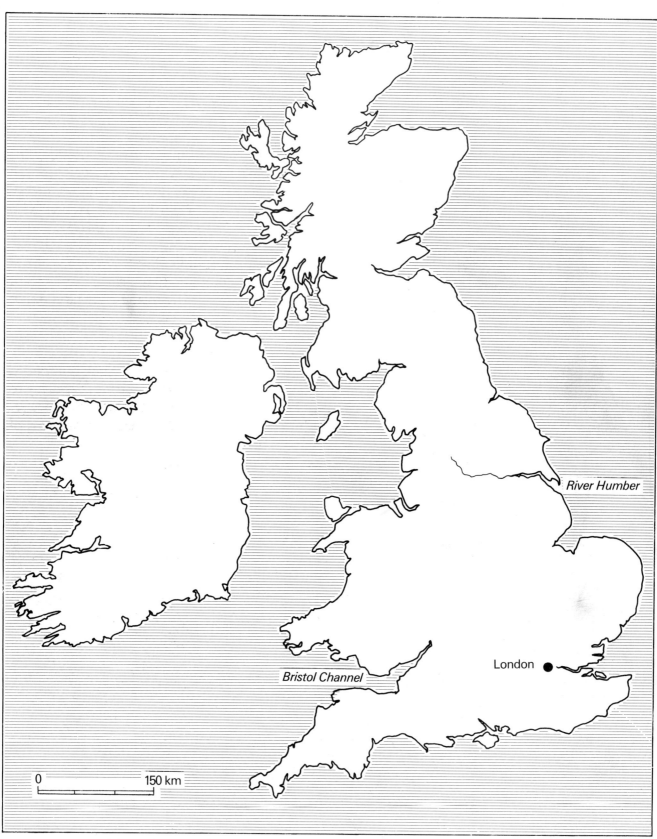

River Humber

Bristol Channel

London ●

0         150 km

▲ Outline map of Britain for use in study sections

# 1 The Romans in Britain

## Boudica's revolt

### The death of Prasutagus

Boudica was a widow. Her husband, Prasutagus, who died in AD 59, had been king of a British tribe called the Iceni. He had ruled his people for many years. During his reign the Romans had conquered southern **Britain**, but they had allowed Prasutagus to keep his land and go on ruling his tribe.

When her husband died, Boudica thought that the Romans would let her rule in his place with her two daughters. But, without telling Boudica, the Romans decided to take over the lands of the Iceni for themselves.

### Boudica quarrels with the Romans

Soon after Prasutagus died, Roman officials arrived. They ignored Boudica and began to take land from her relatives and friends to give to Romans. They also told the people that they would have to pay higher taxes to Rome.

Boudica was very angry. She was a strong and determined woman, and as Queen of the Iceni she expected to be treated with respect. She complained, but the Roman officials refused to listen to her. They only paid attention to orders from Rome, and when Boudica argued with them they called in soldiers who dragged her away, flogged her and assaulted her daughters.

Boudica was furious. The Romans had stolen her kingdom and humiliated her. She vowed to take her revenge by driving these invaders out of Britain once and for all.

### The rebel army gathers

Boudica's chance came a year later. Suetonius, the Roman governor, took most of his army to fight in Wales. As he marched west Boudica set off on a journey round her territory and that of

▼ Southern Britain at the time of Boudica

a neighbouring tribe, the Trinovantes, trying to persuade men to leave their homes for a few months and join her army to drive out the Romans.

Everywhere she went she found plenty of recruits. Some believed that Boudica had been badly treated. Many hated the Romans because Roman officials had taken their land or suddenly demanded huge sums of money. Others resented having to pay taxes to the Romans. In particular they hated having to pay for the temple of Claudius in Camulodunum (now Colchester), where the Romans worshipped their emperor. Many men joined her army because they loved fighting, and looked forward to bringing back valuable plunder from the new towns that the Romans were building in Britain.

## The attack on Camulodunum

Within a few weeks Boudica had an army of 70,000 men. With this huge force she advanced towards Camulodunum, a prosperous town with streets of wooden houses and shops. The only stone building was the brand-new temple of Claudius. There were hardly any soldiers in the town, and when Boudica arrived she found that most of the inhabitants had fled from their homes and barricaded themselves in the temple.

For two days Boudica's army rampaged through Camulodunum. They broke into shops and houses, and stole food, drink, clothing and jewellery. Then they turned on the hated temple, battered down the doors and burst in. Laughing and shouting, they began to kill the people who had taken shelter there. Men, women and children were hacked to pieces. Nobody was spared. Then Boudica's men set fire to the town and left. Three days earlier Camulodunum had been a bustling town. Now it was a smoking ruin.

## The rebels seize Londinium

From Camulodunum the rebels turned towards Londinium (London), 85 km away. As they marched across the countryside a Roman messenger rode off to Wales as fast as he could, to tell Suetonius what was happening.

▲ British war chariots were mostly wood. They were light and easy to handle

▼ Londinium burns. Most of the buildings were timber, like the shops on the right. The roads were gravel

The Roman governor was in Anglesey, where he had just captured a British stronghold. As soon as he heard the news, Suetonius galloped to Londinium with his cavalry, leaving his infantry to follow as fast as they could.

When Suetonius reached Londinium, Boudica and her huge army were very near. He knew that if he stayed he and his troops would be overwhelmed. He ordered the citizens to leave the town, and rode back towards Wales to link up with his infantry.

So when Boudica reached Londinium there was no one to defend it. Her army set fire to every building, and killed all the people they could find, leaving their hacked and torn bodies lying in the smouldering ruins. Then they moved north to Verulamium (now St Albans) and did the same. In a few weeks they had destroyed the three largest towns in Britain, and had killed more than 60,000 people.

### The rebels meet the Roman army

Boudica now set out to search for Suetonius and his army. About half-way to Wales she found them—a small force of about 10,000 men drawn up at the end of a sloping valley.

When Boudica's men saw how small the Roman army was, they felt sure they would easily sweep it aside. Many of them had their wives and children with them, and had brought wagons loaded with booty from the towns they had conquered. They quickly put the wagons in a long straight line behind them. Their wives and children clambered up on them to get a good view.

Then, swinging their swords, the ragged army charged up the valley. But the Roman infantry stood firm. The rebels hesitated. At once the Roman infantry advanced, shoulder to shoulder. The rebels began to retreat. Immediately the Roman cavalry charged down on them, driving them back to the wagons where their wives and children were watching.

The rebels were trapped, and the Romans showed no mercy. One Roman historian said that they killed 80,000 men, women and children, and lost only 400 of their own men.

Boudica escaped from the battlefield, but died before the Romans could capture her. Her attempt to drive the Romans out of Britain had failed. They were to remain for nearly 400 years.

# Studying the story

## How do we know?

**The eye witness and the historian**

We know the story of Boudica because a Roman historian called Tacitus wrote it down. In AD 97 he wrote a short account of Boudica's rebellion. Later, in AD 112, he told the story in more detail.

Tacitus himself never visited Britain, but his wife's father, Agricola, was there when the rebellion broke out. At the time, he was a young officer in the army of Suetonius.

The story of Boudica that you have just read is based on what Agricola told Tacitus many years later.

1 How many years after the rebellion did Tacitus first write about it?
2 Agricola was with Suetonius during the rebellion. Name two events described in the story
   (a) that he could have seen for himself.
   (b) that he could not have seen for himself.
3 If Tacitus had wanted to check that Agricola's memory was accurate, can you suggest how he might have done this?

**The archaeological remains**

The British Isles have been inhabited for thousands of years. People from every age have left remains that give us clues about their lives. Many of these remains lie buried in the earth, still waiting to be discovered. Others have been dug up or **excavated** by archaeologists. Sometimes we can use these remains to check or **verify** that what we have read in a story really happened. Which statements in the story of Boudica do the following archaeological remains help us to verify?

*Colchester (Camulodunum)*
1 The **podium** or stone foundations of a large Roman temple built in about AD 50.
2 The remains of a pottery shop that was burnt down in a great fire in about AD 60.

*London (Londinium) and St Albans (Verulamium)*
3 A layer of ash dating from about AD 60, covering the area where the Roman town would have stood.

## Understanding what happened

**The main events of the rebellion**

The events below are not in the correct order. Re-write them in the order in which they happened.

1 Boudica leads a rebellion against the Romans and destroys Camulodunum.
2 Suetonius and the Roman army go to Wales.
3 Boudica's rebels destroy Londinium and Verulamium and kill the townspeople.
4 Suetonius hears of the rebellion, rides with the cavalry to try to save Londinium, but abandons the town.
5 The Romans and Britons meet in battle. The Romans win. Boudica flees and, later, dies.
6 King Prasutagus dies and the Romans take over the Kingdom of the Iceni.

**The reasons why the Britons rebelled**

The Romans had let Prasutagus stay in power.

1 What power did the Romans take away from Boudica after the death of Prasutagus?
2 How did the Romans use their power to ill-treat
   (a) Boudica?
   (b) her friends and relatives?
   (c) the ordinary tribesmen?
   (d) the Trinovantes?
3 The Romans depended on the army to enforce their power.
   (a) Where did Suetonius take most of the army?
   (b) Why did the Iceni then think it was safe for them to rebel?

**The final battle**

No one knows where the armies of Suetonius and Boudica fought their battle. We believe it was somewhere along the road that ran from Londinium to Wales.

Look at the map of roads on page 26.

1 (a) Name the road that runs from Londinium to Wales.

(b) Where, along this road, did the battle probably take place?

2 The Britons thought they would easily defeat the Romans. Why did they think this?

3 The British tribesmen spent most of their time farming. The Romans were trained soldiers.

(a) Find examples from the battle to show the superior military skill of the Romans.

(b) Why were the rebels unable to go on fighting after this battle?

# Further work

**One story—different versions**

1 (a) From memory write the story of Boudica. Mention who she was, why she rebelled and what happened to her.

(b) Compare what you have written with the story in this book. Is your account

not very accurate?

fairly accurate?

completely accurate?

(c) Why must a historian be accurate?

2 Tell the story from the point of view of a Roman—you could choose Suetonius, or the messenger, or one of the cavalry. Make it clear which events you saw for yourself and which you learnt about from other people.

3 There is no account of the rebellion by a Briton who lived at the time.

(a) Can you suggest why not?

(b) Imagine that a British tribesman who had rebelled told his story many years later. Mention his reasons for rebelling, his part in the capture of London and how he fought in the last battle between Suetonius and Boudica.

**Reading aloud**

Tacitus wrote some of his books to be read aloud to an audience. The audience applauded at the end of each section.

Choose the best version of the story of Boudica written by a member of your class. Give this to a team of readers to prepare and read to the class, who form the audience.

**Speeches**

Divide into groups of four. Give one person in each group one of the following speeches to prepare:

1 Boudica's speech to the tribesmen when she was organising the rebellion.

2 The messenger giving the news of the rebellion to Suetonius.

3 A citizen of Londinium begging Suetonius not to abandon the city.

The speech should last about one minute. Choose the best speaker in each group to make the speech to the class.

**What do you think?**

1 Choose one incident when the Romans were brutal to the Britons and one when the Britons treated the Romans savagely. Explain why, in each case, they may have behaved in this way.

**Drawing**

1 Draw the Roman soldier on page 8.

2 Draw a map of Britain at the time of Boudica's rebellion. Show

(a) the territory of the Iceni and the Trinovantes;

(b) the three towns;

(c) the road from Londinium to Wales;

(d) the probable site of the battle.

3 Draw a strip cartoon of five or six pictures to illustrate the main events in the story of Boudica.

5

# The Romans conquer Britannia

## The early history of Rome

By AD 60 when Boudica rebelled against them, the Romans already had a history going back more than 500 years. They came from central Italy, and took their name from the city of Rome which was their capital.

The Romans were quite a small tribe, but they had a well-trained army. They gradually captured more and more land until by 175 BC they ruled the whole of central and southern Italy. By 100 BC they ruled most of the north coast of the Mediterranean, including southern **Gaul.**

## The Romans learn about Britain

In 100 BC most Romans thought that no one lived beyond the north coast of Gaul. They knew that beyond it there was a wild and stormy sea. Some had heard rumours that there was a cold, foggy, barren land on the other side of this sea, but they took it for granted that nobody lived there. It was too far north and too cold.

By 50 BC they knew better. In 57 BC the Roman general, Julius Caesar, defeated the tribes of northern Gaul. And there, across the water, he and his men could see the northern land, which they called **Britannia.**

They discovered that it was a rich country with tin and silver mines, and farms which produced a good harvest of wheat. They also found out that the people who lived in Britannia were friendly with the tribes in Gaul that Caesar had just conquered. In 56 BC one of these tribes rebelled, and fighting men came from Britannia to help them against the Romans. This annoyed Caesar, and when he had crushed the revolt he crossed the northern sea to teach the Britons a lesson.

## Caesar's invasions

In September 55 BC Caesar landed with a small army on the south coast of Britannia. A British army tried to drive him back, but the Romans defeated it. Then a great storm sprang up and destroyed many Roman ships. This alarmed Caesar, and as soon as the weather was calm again, he packed his troops into the remaining ships and sailed back to Gaul.

In 54 BC Caesar returned with a much larger army. He fought his way north, crossed the river Thames and captured a British stronghold. He then offered to leave Britannia, provided the Britons made a treaty of friendship with Rome, paid a yearly **tribute** of money, and handed over hostages who would be killed if the treaty was broken. The Britons agreed. They made the treaty, and Caesar took his troops back to Gaul.

## Claudius and Britannia

For nearly 100 years there was peace between Britannia and Rome. The tribes of south-east Britannia sold cattle, leather, corn, gold and slaves to Gaul and in return bought wine, pottery and iron. Camulodunum, the British port on the east coast, grew and prospered. Today Colchester stands on its site.

At first the rulers of the south east were careful not to upset the Romans, but in AD 40 the most powerful of them, Cunobelin, died. He left his kingdom to his two sons, who at once began to invade the territory of other tribes in the area.

Some of these tribes were friendly with the Romans, and asked them for help. The Roman emperor, Claudius, decided to put an end to all this trouble. He would invade Britannia and make it a Roman province, part of the Roman Empire.

## The invading army

By summer AD 43 Claudius had collected an army of 40,000 men in northern Gaul. In the past the Romans had beaten every army in Europe, and Aulus Plautius, who commanded the invading army in AD 43, was certain that he could defeat the Britons as well.

His infantry, who fought on foot, were the best fighting men. They all had metal armour with helmets and wooden shields to protect them, and each carried two **javelins** and a short sword.

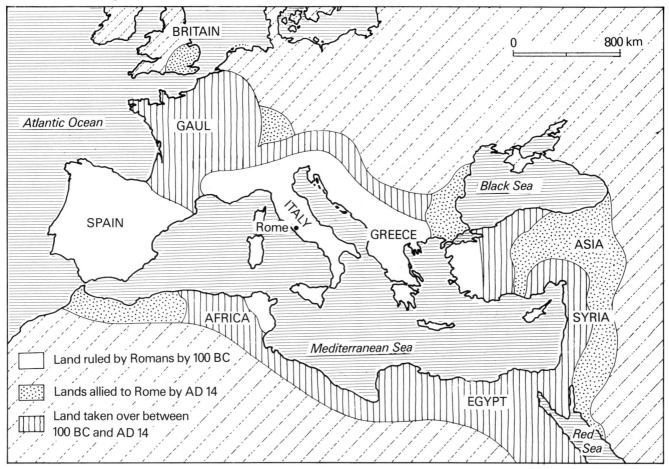

Land ruled by Romans by 100 BC

Lands allied to Rome by AD 14

Land taken over between 100 BC and AD 14

The infantry were very well trained. In battle they first threw their javelins at the enemy. Then they drew their swords, and with their shields held in front of them, charged forward at a steady trot. When they reached the enemy they tried to knock them off balance with their shields and stab them with their swords.

The Romans had other troops to help the infantry. Cavalry mounted on horses charged the enemy with spears. Slingers, stone-throwers and bowmen showered them with stones and arrows.

### The invasion begins

One summer night in AD 43 a huge Roman fleet set sail from Gaul. By morning the ships were at anchor at Richborough in Kent, and the army was on shore setting up camp. Some of the soldiers put up leather tents in neat lines. Others dug ditches and made a wooden **stockade** to protect the camp from attack. There was no sign of the Britons.

Aulus Plautius spent several days at Richborough. His men built wooden store-houses and filled them with supplies. Then the army set out, marching west. They marched for several days until they came to the river Medway. And on the opposite bank they saw the British army.

### The British army

The best British troops were charioteers who were armed with long swords. These men rode into battle on small, light, two-wheeled chariots pulled by ponies. Each chariot contained two men—the warrior and his driver.

Sometimes the warriors stayed in their chariots to fight, striking out at any of the enemy within reach. But more often they jumped down and ran at their foes, swinging vicious blows with their long swords. When they were tired or in danger they jumped back into their chariots, and were driven away to a safe spot until they felt ready to fight again.

▲ The Roman soldier's helmet and armour were made of bronze. His sword was iron

## The battle at the Medway

As they stood on the bank of the Medway, the Britons felt quite safe. They did not see how the Romans could cross the river and clamber up the bank while they were there to push them back.

On the other bank the Romans brought up carts loaded with wooden platforms to the river. Then, away to one side, a number of Roman soldiers waded into the water and began to swim across. The British charioteers turned and drove along the bank to stop them landing.

Immediately the rest of the Romans set to work. Quickly they joined some of the platforms together, and pushed them out into the river. In this way they made a number of floating bridges. The infantry streamed across to the other bank and lined up side by side.

The British charioteers saw what was happening and galloped back along the top of the bank to sweep the Romans into the river. The Romans waited quietly and then, when the Britons were quite close, threw their javelins straight at the ponies. Many ponies were killed or injured, and the Britons jumped down and dashed at the Roman line shouting and swinging their swords.

But with their heads down and their shields held in front of them, the Romans were like a wall of wood and metal. The British swords glanced off their helmets or stuck in their shields. And all the time the Romans stabbed at the Britons with their short swords.

Soon the Britons grew tired. When this happened the Romans moved forward a few metres, making room for more men behind them.

The Britons thought that if the Romans were defeated on the Medway they would give up their invasion and go back to Gaul. So the British troops went on fighting. Once they sent the centre of the Roman line reeling back almost to the river, but they never broke through.

After two days' fighting many Britons had been killed, and those who were left were tired and hungry. They realised that they could not defeat the Romans. So they retreated, leaving behind them dead and dying men and ponies, broken swords and smashed chariots. The Roman army moved on.

## The conquest of Britannia

The battle on the Medway was the hardest that the Romans had to fight in their conquest of Britannia. They moved steadily west and north. Even huge hill-forts protected by deep ditches and high banks of earth could not stop them.

To attack these forts the Romans used **ballistas**, which could throw rocks weighing 50 kg, and catapults which fired sharp metal bolts. These bolts killed anyone who showed his head above the **ramparts**, and the stones from the ballistas soared over the defences and crashed down on the men packed inside.

Meanwhile the infantry held their shields over their heads to protect them, and battered at the gates of the fort until they smashed their way through. In all, the Romans captured twenty British hill-forts.

▼ Maiden castle in Dorset was one of the strongest hill-forts captured by the Romans. When it was excavated the skeleton of a man was found with a Roman catapult bolt in his back

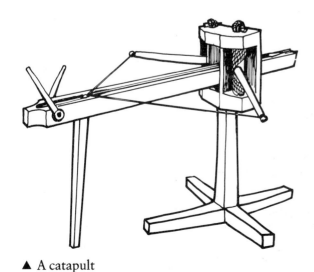

▲ A catapult

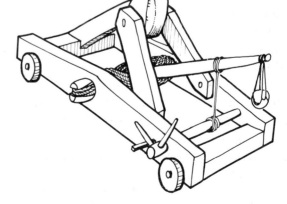

▲ A ballista

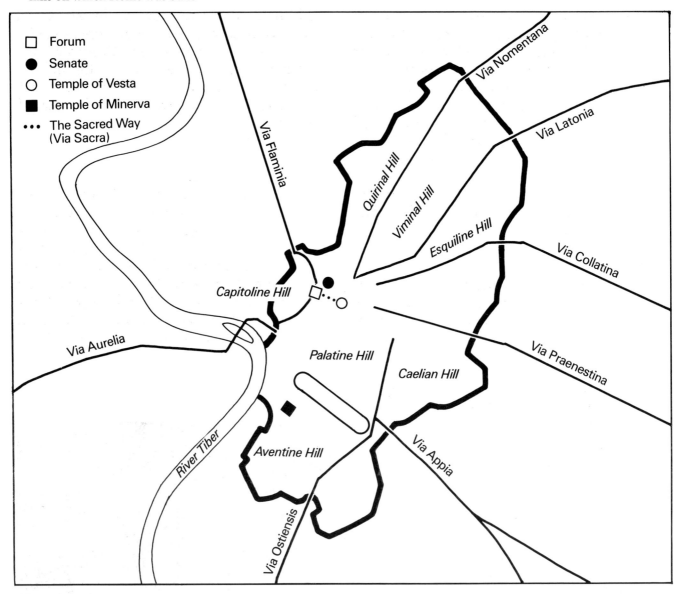

It seemed that nothing could stop the Romans, and many tribes surrendered to them without a fight because they knew that the Romans would defeat them. By AD 47 the Romans controlled the whole country south of a line from the river Humber to the Bristol Channel (see the map facing page 1).

### The first Roman towns

As soon as they had taken over an area, the Romans built towns. Rome itself (see the plan) was the model for all the towns in the empire. By AD 60 there were three towns in Britannia. Camulodunum (now Colchester) was the oldest, with a rich stone temple dedicated to the Emperor Claudius who had visited the town to accept the surrender of a number of British chiefs. Many of the citizens were retired soldiers. They lived in pleasant wooden houses, and had shops where they could buy goods imported from the rest of the Roman Empire.

Another important town was founded at Verulamium, the modern St Albans, while on the Thames a bustling new port named Londinium was growing up. The Romans were pleased with what they had achieved in Britannia. Boudica's rebellion came as a terrible shock to them, but once it was over they went on moving steadily north.

# The Roman army in the north

The Romans never conquered the whole of Britain. In AD 84 an army commanded by the governor, Agricola, advanced almost as far north as Inverness in Scotland and defeated the local tribes in a great battle, but then the emperor in Rome took some of his troops away to fight against rebels in Gaul. So Agricola had to retreat and leave Scotland to be ruled by its own native chiefs. If they had left the Romans in peace all might have been well, but again and again the Scots invaded the northern part of Britannia, killing the inhabitants and stealing crops and animals.

## Hadrian's wall

In AD 122 the Emperor Hadrian visited Britannia. He decided to divide the Roman province from the rest of Britain by building a wall from the mouth of the Tyne in the east to the Solway firth in the west (see page 12). By AD 130 the wall was finished. It was 118 km long, 5 m high and between 2 m and 3 m thick. Every one and a half kilometres there was a gate through the wall guarded by a small tower, and every half kilometre there was a watch tower from which soldiers could keep an eye on what was happening to the north.

## The fort at Housesteads

The troops who guarded the wall lived in seventeen forts spaced out along its whole length. These forts were all built to much the same pattern. Housesteads, which stood about half-way along the wall, covered an area measuring about 190 m by 116 m, surrounded by a stone wall with a ditch and rampart. It had four gates which had towers on each side to protect them. Housesteads was easy to defend.

▼ A model of the fort at Chesters on Hadrian's wall. In Roman times it probably looked like this

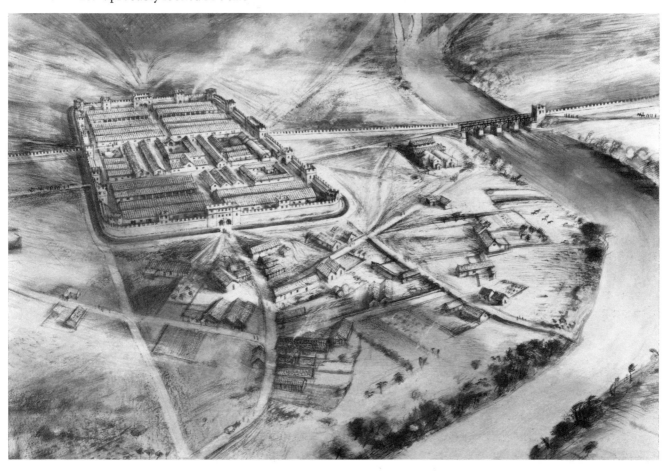

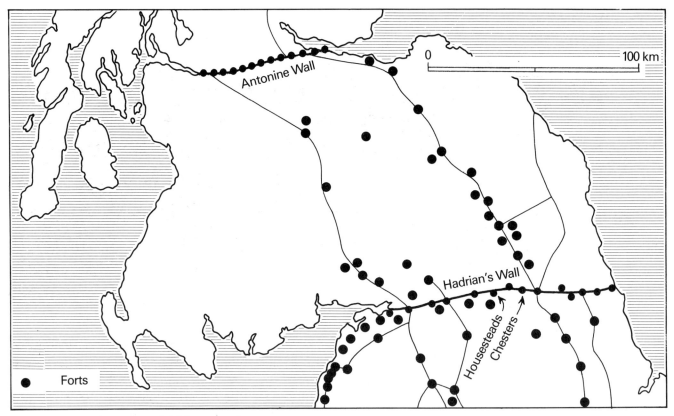

▲ There was a vast area of wild country between Hadrian's wall and the Antonine wall. The Romans never really controlled this area

▼ This plan of Housesteads shows the layout of the main buildings

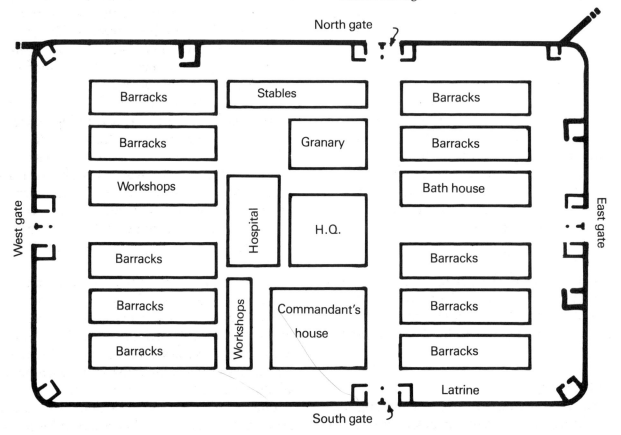

## The headquarters

At the centre of the fort stood the headquarters building, which contained the offices where the clerks worked. They wrote dispatches, ordered supplies, recorded all the money received and spent, and kept a detailed diary of all the duties that the troops stationed in the fort carried out.

The headquarters also contained an assembly yard big enough to hold all the troops in the fort, a strong-room where money was kept, and a small temple containing the **standards** which the troops carried into battle.

## The commander's house

Next to the headquarters there was a large house built round a central courtyard. This belonged to the commander of the fort. He was appointed by the governor of the province, and came from a rich landowning family. His wife and family lived with him, and there were slaves to look after them. He spent most of his time working in the headquarters building.

## The hospital

On the other side of the headquarters there was a hospital, where sick and wounded soldiers were looked after by a medical officer, helped by a number of troops who had been trained as nurses.

## Other buildings

The rest of the camp was filled with long narrow buildings. Most were barrack rooms where the soldiers ate and slept. Some were granaries holding enough wheat and barley to keep the fort supplied for many months. There were stables for the horses, sheds for the carts and wagons, and also a few workshops.

## Life on the northern frontier

There were more than a thousand soldiers at Housesteads. Most of them had been born within a few kilometres of the fort. Many were sons of soldiers who had served at Housesteads in years gone by. They had joined the army at about the age of twenty, and had signed on to serve for twenty-five years.

They had a busy life at the fort. Three times a month they went out on a training march of 30 km. This helped to keep them fit. Occasionally a few of them were sent to patrol the country north of the wall to make sure that everything there was peaceful. Sometimes two or three hundred went out with tents and weapons to pitch camp several kilometres from the fort, where they spent a few days fighting mock battles.

Even when the soldiers were in the barracks there was plenty to do. They had to collect fuel, clean weapons, scrub the barracks, clean out the lavatories and muck out the stables. Soldiers who worked as clerks, nurses and craftsmen did not have to do any cleaning and polishing, but all the rest had to take their turn.

Life in the army was very strict. If they did not do as they were told soldiers could be beaten, fined, put on reduced rations or discharged from the army. But in other ways the soldiers at Housesteads were very well off. They were paid regularly. They had good food with plenty of meat, milk, cheese, bread, wine and fruit.

In their spare time they could go to the **vicus**—a small village just outside the gates of the fort. Here there was a bath-house. There were also inns, shops and a number of houses where the wives and children of the soldiers lived. Most of the shopkeepers were retired soldiers who had served the whole of their twenty-five years at Housesteads.

## The Antonine wall
For most of the time the Romans were in Britain, Hadrian's wall marked their northern frontier. In about AD 140, however, Roman troops invaded southern Scotland and built another wall, this time of turf (see the map on page 12).

The new wall, which stretched from the firth of Forth to the firth of Clyde—a distance of about 60 km—was built on the orders of the Emperor Antoninus. It was not occupied for long. In about AD 155 there was a rebellion in Britannia, and the troops who had been guarding the Antonine wall were brought south to crush it.

Before they left the wall they destroyed their forts so that they would be of no use to their enemies. Two or three years later some of the troops returned, but in about AD 160 they abandoned the Antonine wall for good and went back to the forts of Hadrian's wall.

▲ A stone water-tank at Housesteads. The Romans and their successors sharpened weapons and tools on the sides of the tank. This has worn them into hollows

## Use your imagination

### A soldier's life

1 Caradoc, a British tribesman, has joined the Roman army. Write an account of his first year at Housesteads.
*Things to write about:*
Caradoc's weapons and armour (What were they like?)
His life in the barracks at Housesteads
His reasons for thinking that life in the army was better than being with his tribe
(Think of when you started at a new school or joined a club, and how you liked it once you had got used to the way that things were done there.)

2 Marcus has served twenty-five years in the Roman army. Write an account of the year when he retires and gets married.
*Things to write about:*
Marcus' last training march with the new recruits
Marcus marries a British woman and holds a wedding feast
The shop that Marcus and his wife set up in the vicus
(Think of something you did for the last time before your life changed.)

3 Quintus, the new Roman commander, has arrived at Housesteads with his wife, Julia, and their sons, Gaius and Lucius. Write an account of the family's first day at Housesteads.
*Things to write about:*
Quintus inspects his headquarters and sees the clerks at work
The family's living quarters (What were they like? What did Julia think of them?)
Gaius and Lucius explore the granaries and workshops
(Think of an interesting place you know, and how you explored it for the first time.)

## Measuring time

### Measuring forward in time
When were you born? How old are you today? Answer exactly in years, months and days.
   As you can see, the date of your birth gives you a point to measure from. You will use this measurement all your life as you move *forward* in time.

### Measuring backwards in time
Do you remember the Battle of Britain in 1940? No—it happened before you were born. You are using your birthday to measure from again, moving back in time.

### Measuring from the birth of Jesus
Historians in our part of the world measure from the birth of Jesus Christ.

BC means so many years before the birth of Christ.
AD means so many years after the birth of Christ.
Starting from this point, we can measure forward or backward in time.

### Historians measure long periods of time
Think of time as a ruler divided into sections:

a millennium is   1,000 years
a century is       100 years
a decade is         10 years

When we pass the year AD 2000 we shall be entering the third millennium of the Christian era, or period measured from the birth of Christ.

→

## The Romans conquer Britain: a time chart

| Era | Date | Century | Important event |
|---|---|---|---|
| BC | 57 | | British tribes help the Gauls to fight Julius Caesar |
| | 55 | I | Julius Caesar invades Britain |
| | 54 | | Julius Caesar invades Britain again |
| AD | 43 | | Emperor Claudius invades Britain |
| | | | The Romans control all Britain south of the Humber to the Bristol channel |
| | 84 | | Boudica's rebellion |
| | | | Agricola fails to conquer Scotland |
| | | | Emperor Hadrian's wall is built in north Britain |
| | 140 | 2 | Emperor Antoninus builds a wall further north |
| | | | Roman troops leave the Antonine wall to fight rebels in the south of Britain |
| | 160 | | Hadrian's wall marks the northern frontier of Roman Britain |

## Making time charts

When we study history, we move around the past in our minds. Time charts help us to do this.

1 (a) Copy the chart above.
(b) Fill in the spaces in the *Date* and *Century* columns. You will find the dates you need in the section *The Romans in Britain* on pages 1 to 16.

## Using your time chart

1 Write out these sentences, filling in the spaces. To find the answers, read across the chart from left to right.
(a) In the year 55 BC Julius Caesar _____ Britain for the first time.
(b) By AD 160, Hadrian's _____ marked the Romans' _____ frontier in Britain.
2 Write out these sentences, filling in the spaces. To find the answers, read down the century column.
(a) In the _____ century AD Boudica led a rebellion against the Romans.
(b) In the _____ century AD there was another rebellion in the south of Britain.
3 Answer these questions by reading *down* the date column and *across* to the important event column.

(a) How did the British tribes help the Gauls in 57 BC?
(b) Which part of Britain did Agricola fail to conquer in AD 84?
4 *True or false?*
Use the section *Measuring time* and your time chart to find out whether these statements are true or false.
(a) The Emperor Claudius came to Britain nearly a century after Julius Caesar's first invasion.
(b) Two decades after the Emperor Antoninus built a wall the Roman troops withdrew to Hadrian's wall.

## Time chart quizzes

1 *Down and across*
Divide the class into two teams. Allow everyone five minutes to make up an 'across', 'down', or 'down and across' question and write it on a slip of paper. Give the slips to the question master. You may look at the time chart, but you have only five seconds to find the answer.
2 *True or false?*
Use the same rules as for 'Down and across', but make up 'True or false?' questions.

# Life in Britannia

## Town life in the second century

**The port of Londinium**

As soon as Boudica's rebellion was over the Romans had begun to rebuild Londinium. The town was important because at Londinium the Thames was easy to bridge, and the water was deep enough for sea-going ships to sail right into the middle of the town.

The ships brought cargoes of pottery, glass-ware, spices, figs, olives, dates and wine. These goods were eventually loaded onto wagons and taken by road to towns all over southern Britannia. The boats were then loaded with Cornish tin, lead from Somerset, iron from Kent and wheat from local farms, which were shipped off to pay for the imports.

**Merchants and their houses**

All this trade meant that there were many wealthy merchants in Londinium. Most of them were Britons who had come to live and work in the town. The merchants lived in large houses. Some of these had as many as thirty rooms built round a central courtyard. Stone was scarce, so only the very rich could afford to use it for building. Most houses were made of a timber framework with walls of mud brick or wattle and daub. This consisted of lengths of flexible wood woven together to form a screen which was then covered with layers of mud or plaster (a mixture of lime and sand).

Inside the house the walls were covered with plaster, painted white or pink. In some rooms, the walls had pictures of plants and animals painted on them, and in a few of the richest houses there were **mosaics** on the floors. But mosaics were very expensive, and most floors

▲ Londinium as it probably looked before the fire of about AD 130. The forum and basilica are on the hill above the bridge over the Thames. The governor's palace stands at the mouth of the Wall brook. The Cripplegate fort is on the other side of the stream. The city walls were not built until after the fire

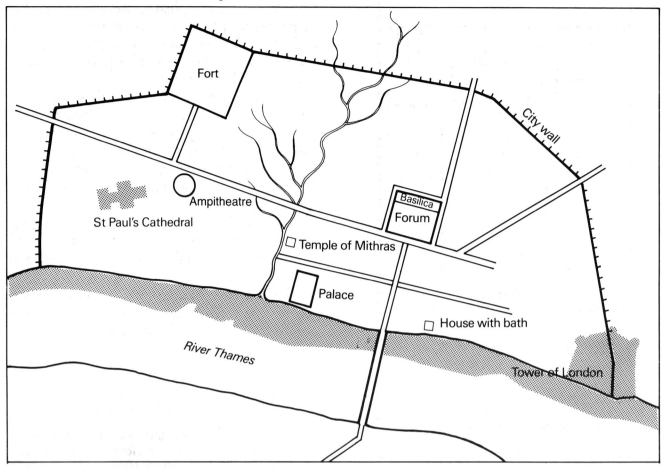

were plaster or cement.

Houses were roofed with red clay tiles, and kept warm by a central heating system which circulated hot air from a furnace through channels under the floors. Many houses had their own water supply. Wells were dug deep in the clay, and their shafts were lined with old wine barrels.

Some houses had gardens in which peas, cabbages, carrots, cucumbers, strawberries and raspberries were grown.

### The merchant's household

The merchant's wife looked after his house and garden. She had slaves to help her. They worked in the garden, cleaned the house, stoked the furnace, cooked the meals and looked after the children.

Slaves also helped the merchant in his business. When he went down to the river to buy goods from the ships that had arrived, a slave went with him. The slave carried a wooden tablet covered with wax, and made a note of everything the merchant bought on it, using a

metal spike about the size of a modern ballpoint pen.

Other slaves then carried the goods to be stored until the merchant found someone who would buy them and take them away to sell in some other town.

### A dinner party

Rich merchants often entertained their friends by giving a dinner party. Before the guests arrived the merchant and his wife both put on their best clothes, and his wife made up her face.

She kept make-up colours in small clay jars. Using a long-handled spoon she took a little from each jar and mixed it all together in a small bowl. When the colour of the mixture looked right, she applied it carefully to her face, checking in a polished bronze mirror to make sure that it suited her.

Meanwhile in the kitchen the slaves might be cooking a hare for the main course. First they scalded it with boiling water, and then baked it in a shallow pan, keeping it well covered with olive oil to stop it drying out.

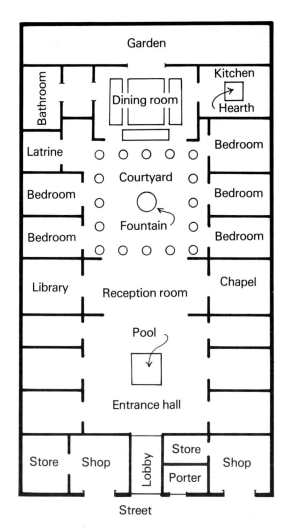

While it was cooking they prepared a sauce from wine, oil, salt, fish sauce, onions, garlic, celery seed, and herbs such as lovage, savory and rue. When the hare was nearly done they poured the sauce over it. This gave the meat a very strong flavour.

When all the guests had arrived the merchant and his wife led the way to the dining room, where they all lounged on long chairs set round the table. They began the meal with oysters, then had the hare served with peas and carrots. Finally, they took their pick from bowls of cherries and plums.

All through the meal they had plenty of wine to drink. They were waited on by slaves, and were entertained as they ate by musicians and dancing girls.

Rich families had a meal of meat or fish served with a spicy sauce and vegetables every day, but poorer people often had to make do

◄ This town house had a dining room, bedrooms, a kitchen, a courtyard and servants' quarters

▼ The stone-paved floor of this room at Housesteads was laid on top of the pillars. Hot air from a furnace on the left circulated under the floor, and escaped up a small chimney on the right

▲ A British man in Roman times

▲ A British woman in Roman times

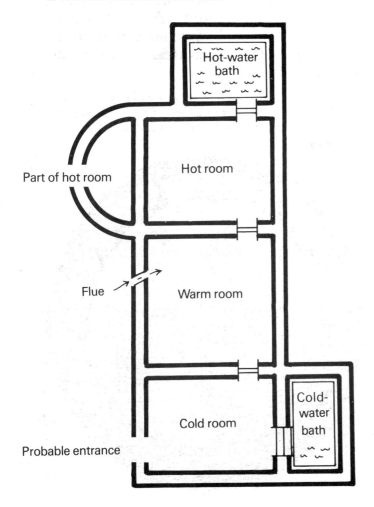

◀ The bath-house at Cheapside was small. Later, larger baths were built in Londinium

with bread or porridge. The Romans had no sugar; they used honey to sweeten their food.

## The Roman bath-house

None of the merchants' houses in Londinium had baths. Instead there was a public bath-house in Cheapside. This consisted of several rooms heated to different temperatures by an underfloor heating system.

Roman baths took anything up to two hours, and merchants often used the time to discuss business deals. Men and women both visited the baths. Sometimes they could take baths together, but in many bath-houses this was against the rules and they had to go at different times.

First the bathers entered a cold room where they undressed. Then they went into a warm room where they rubbed their bodies with oil and sat and sweated, chatting to their friends. Next they went into the hottest room, where they removed the mixture of oil, sweat and dirt from their skins with metal scrapers. Finally

▲ The remains of the amphitheatre at Dorchester in Dorset. Where do you think the audience sat?

they made their way back to the cold room where they plunged into a bath of cold water before getting dressed and leaving.

## Entertainments in Londinium

In 1988 archaeologists discovered the remains of an **amphitheatre** where travelling bands of gladiators came and staged fights. The men were armed with swords, so these fights were very dangerous, and often gladiators were injured or even killed.

The Romans loved violent shows, and when there were no gladiators they used to watch cock-fights or dogs tormenting a bear. They also went hunting for deer, hares, wild boar, badgers and woodcock. These all ran wild in the woods that surrounded the town.

▲ The man who made this tile scratched some words on it while it was still soft: 'Austalis dibus XIII vagatur sib cotidim' ('Austalis has been going off on his own every day for the past fortnight')

## The craftsmen of Londinium

The merchants were the richest people in Londinium. There were also many craftsmen and shopkeepers in the town. A couple of mills stood on the banks of the Wall brook where millers ground corn into flour, which they sold to bakers who made loaves and cakes to sell in their shops.

At Aldgate there was a slaughterhouse where butchers killed cattle, sheep and pigs, cut them into joints and sold them.

There were also blacksmiths, goldsmiths, tailors, shoemakers, tile-makers, builders, spinners, weavers and potters. Their workshops were usually built onto their houses. It was a busy, crowded town.

## The governor and his staff

Many Roman officials lived and worked in Londinium. The most important was the governor, who lived in a great palace with huge rooms where he could entertain important visitors to the province. The governor was in charge of the whole of Britannia. He commanded the army, controlled the courts of law, made sure that the chiefs of the various tribes did as they were told, and decided which roads should be made.

▼ Mosaic pictures were made from small pieces of stone of different colours set in cement. They were difficult to make. This one was found on a Roman site in London in 1803

To help him the governor had a staff of about 200 people. The most important of these was the procurator, who was in charge of collecting taxes in the province.

To protect the city the governor had a thousand troops, who were stationed at Cripplegate, in a barracks about the same size as the fort at Housesteads.

◄ The head of the statue of Hadrian which once stood in the forum. It was found in the Thames near London Bridge in 1834

▼ A plan of Londinium's forum and basilica

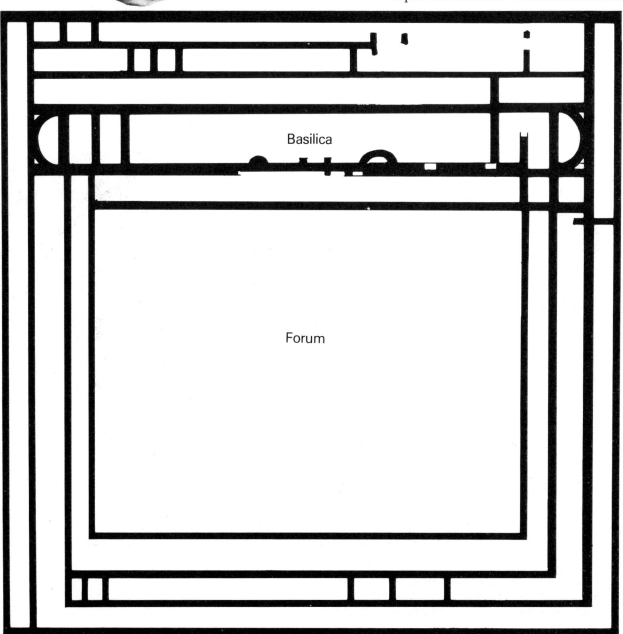

Basilica

Forum

## The basilica and the forum

Londinium was run by a town council whose offices were in the **forum**, a huge area nearly 170 m square. In the middle of the forum there was an open space which was used for public meetings. In it stood a bronze statue of the Emperor Hadrian, in whose honour the forum had been built in about AD 125.

On three sides the forum was surrounded by shops sheltered by covered walks. On the fourth side stood the **basilica**, which held a large hall for public meetings, a council chamber, offices and a prison.

## Temples and religion

There were several temples in Londinium. The Roman Empire had many gods. Some, like Jupiter, king of the gods, and Mars, the god of war, were worshipped all over the empire. But there were also local gods.

Some aspects of Roman religion seem strange to us today. The Romans often asked their gods to put curses on their enemies. They scratched a curse on one side of a sheet of lead, and then nailed the sheet, with the smooth side showing, onto the god's shrine. One curse found in Londinium begins, 'I curse Tretia Maria and her life and mind and memory and liver and lungs.'

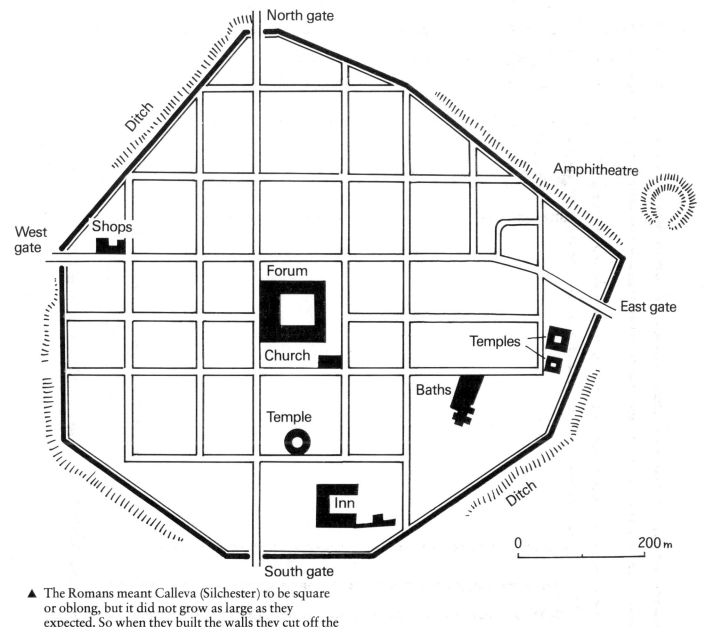

▲ The Romans meant Calleva (Silchester) to be square or oblong, but it did not grow as large as they expected. So when they built the walls they cut off the corners

As a rule the Romans allowed the people they conquered to worship whatever gods they pleased. But they had banned the religion of Druidism. Druids worshipped their gods in groves of holy oaks and mistletoe. They also practised human sacrifice. The Romans disapproved of this, hunted down the Druids, and wiped them out.

For many years the Romans also banned Christianity. They believed that Christians would rather follow Christ's teaching than obey the emperor. But as time went on the Christians were allowed to worship freely, and in AD 324 a Christian, Constantine, became emperor in Rome.

Christianity was especially popular among the poor and churches were built in many towns. By the time the Romans left Britannia in AD 407 the emperor and his officials throughout the empire were Christian, and the Church was more important than the temples.

## Other towns

Londinium was by far the biggest town in Britannia. By AD 130 it had an area of about 130 ha. There were about forty other towns, 40 ha or less in size, and with populations of between 2,000 and 3,000. Most of the inhabitants were British, who enjoyed town life as much as the Romans did.

Most towns were square or oblong though there were exceptions, such as Calleva (see the plan on page 23). They were surrounded by walls to protect them from attack. They usually had four gates, one in the middle of each wall. Every town had a forum and basilica, usually in the middle of the town, and like Londinium had shops, temples, a bath-house and an amphitheatre.

Towns were healthy places. Nearly all of them were supplied with clean water from a nearby stream. Many also had sewers, so that the streets and houses had proper drainage.

## The danger of fire

The greatest danger to Roman towns was fire. Smiths and bakers needed fires for their work, and most large houses had furnaces for their central heating system. If one of these fires spread to the timber framework of the building the whole house was soon destroyed, and if there was any wind the flames spread to other buildings.

In about AD 130 a fire destroyed much of Londinium. The Romans rebuilt only part of it. This was probably because other towns in Britannia were now able to produce more of what they wanted for themselves. So their inhabitants stopped buying goods from Londinium, with the result that some merchants could no longer make a living, and left the city.

## The importance of towns

Towns were very important for the Romans. People from the countryside went into the towns to visit the market where they could sell their crops and buy clothes, tools, furniture and jewellery. If they went to the basilica they could speak to the official who governed the area where they lived. As they walked through the streets they would see the fine houses and the splendid temple. And they would probably think how rich and powerful the Roman Empire was. This was just what the Romans wanted.

## Digging up ancient rubbish

### Valuable rubbish

When a team of archaeologists go treasure-hunting they look for a rubbish dump. To them, the bits and pieces of metal that they dig up are valuable. From a piece of torn leather they can tell the fashion in sandals a thousand years ago. Pieces of broken crockery, put back together again, turn into a long-dead Londoner's best dinner dishes.

### Ancient rubbish dumps

*Where* people throw away their rubbish is as important as *what* they throw away.

When the Romans began to build Londinium, many cloth- and leather-workers came to the new city and set up workshops near the Thames. The **fullers** and **tanners** dug long, deep pits in their yards. Into these pits they put the lengths of woollen cloth or animal skins that had to be soaked and cleaned before they were made up into clothing or leather goods. Later, when these craftsmen moved away, the people of Londinium used the pits as rubbish dumps.

Today, archaeologists mark any new pits they find on a map. In this way they can see where these workers and townsmen once lived.

1 Give an example of something that might be found in an ancient rubbish pit.
2 What might this find tell an archaeologist about the life of people in the past?
3 Give an example of something in *your* dustbin and say what it would tell an archaeologist living two thousand years from now about your life today.

Study the pictures on pages 19 and 28.

1 Which picture shows us that in Roman times
(a) floors were paved with stone?
(b) iron was precious?
2 No one has found more than a scrap of cloth in Britain dating from Roman times. Can you suggest why not?
3 Imagine that a large rubbish pit has been found near the line of a Roman road.
(a) Why would archaeologists suspect that the ruins of a Roman settlement were nearby? They decide where the settlement might have been and begin to excavate.
(b) What remains might they find to show that a Roman forum, a basilica and town houses once stood there?

## Country life and travel

### Roman roads and travellers

The Romans spent a lot of time and money making good roads. These ran straight from one hilltop to the next, linking all the major towns. In Britannia there were about 8,000 km of roads. Most of them led to Londinium where the governor lived.

### Travelling messengers

The Romans needed good roads. The emperor and his advisers in Rome often had to send orders or advice to the governor in Britannia. Messengers galloped over the roads of Italy and Gaul to the coast, crossed the sea in a **galley**, and then rode on to Londinium.

If the message was urgent it was handed from one messenger to another, and travelled the

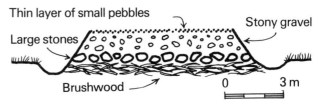

▲ A section through a Roman road. On soft or marshy ground, the Romans built their roads on top of a layer of brushwood. This stopped them sinking

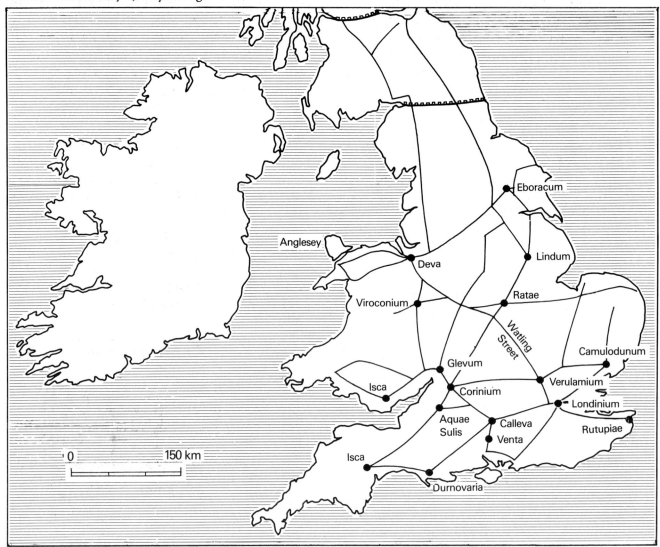

▼ Many roads today follow the course of the Roman roads made nearly 2,000 years ago

1,600 km from Rome to Londinium at a steady 15 kph.

To make sure that their officials were not delayed, the Romans built special changing stations every 20 km along the road. At these stations fresh horses were always ready, and messengers could have a meal and a rest.

### Roads and the army

The Roman army used the road system a lot. They always built a road just behind their frontier, so that if fighting broke out they could move troops to the spot quickly. For instance, there was a road just behind Hadrian's wall.

They also used the other roads to move their troops. In AD 60, when Boudica rebelled, Suetonius galloped with his cavalry along Watling Street from Wales to Londinium.

### Traders on the roads

Traders also travelled the roads. Some carried food and timber from the country to the towns. Others brought imported pottery, wine and oil to inland towns and villas, returning with grain, tin, silver and lead which were exported to other parts of the empire.

Without its roads the Roman Empire could not have survived.

### British farming

Most of the people of Britannia lived in the country. The British tribes lived in villages of round huts, or on isolated farms.

The farmers divided their land into small oblong fields up to 120 m long and more than 30 m wide. Every spring they turned the soil over with a light plough pulled by oxen, and sowed barley, rye, beans or wheat. In the autumn they harvested the grain, dried it and stored it in round pits lined with rushes.

They also kept cows, pigs, sheep and goats. Usually they grew more food than they needed. The Romans took some of the grain to feed their army. The farmers sold the rest and used the money to buy new tools or better animals.

▲ Official messengers used a small carriage like this one

▼ This wagon was used for carrying goods

## Villas

Most British farms were on the hills where the soil was light and easy to plough. Lower down, near the valleys, the Romans set up farms of their own, which were later copied by British farmers. Some were very large—up to 1,000 ha. These farms were called **villas**.

▼ The huts of the hill farmers were crude and uncomfortable compared with the town houses

The owner of a villa lived in a fine house. Some of these houses were made of wood. Others were stone. Most had at least six large rooms. The richest houses were decorated with mosaics and had a private bath-house attached to them. A short distance away from the main house there were barns, stables and living quarters for servants and slaves.

### Frocester Court villa, Gloucestershire

Frocester Court was a typical Roman villa, built about AD 280 in the Vale of Berkeley near the river Severn. The villa buildings included a corn store, a smithy, a dairy, a tannery for making leather and a shed for storing wool.

In front of the house there was a farmyard where hens ran loose, and an orchard where plums, apples, mulberries, cherries and hazelnuts grew. There were also beehives.

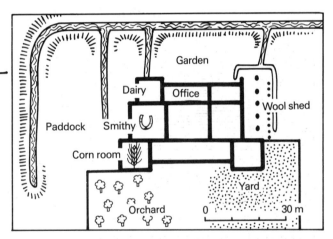

▲ The farm buildings at Frocester were well planned and strongly built

▼ Iron was precious in Roman times. Spades were made of wood, and only the edges were iron

On one side of the buildings there were small fields with horses, ducks and geese, behind the house a vegetable garden was laid out.

The house and its grounds were surrounded by a deep ditch. Beyond it were fertile fields with crops of wheat, barley and oats. The lowest ground was used as cattle pasture. On the slopes of nearby hills flocks of sheep wandered.

The people who lived at Frocester grew almost everything they and their families needed. They had their own bread, meat, beer, milk, cheese, wool, leather and wood. They only had to buy iron, pottery, glass and tools. To pay for these they could sell horses, sheep, cattle, wool, leather and corn.

Frocester was a prosperous place, and in about AD 360 the house was extended. A large new living room was built, and a splendid bath-house with five rooms was added. But about forty years later the villa buildings were burnt down. They were not rebuilt.

## The end of Roman Britain

The villa at Frocester was probably destroyed just after AD 400. Many settlements in Britannia were destroyed at about the same time by raiders from outside the province.

In the north the Picts attacked across Hadrian's wall. Pirates from Ireland crossed the sea to lay waste the south-west, while **Anglo-Saxons** sailed from Germany, landed on the east coast and made their way inland, looting and robbing.

To repel the Saxons the Romans built a number of forts along the south-east coast, and at first their troops were able to drive the raiders away. But raiders were attacking other parts of the empire as well, and in AD 400 they invaded Italy. The government in Rome decided that it was more important to defend Italy than to protect Britannia so they moved many of their troops from Britannia to Rome. Then in AD 407 an army of tribesmen from Germany invaded Gaul, and the commander of the Roman army in Britannia took most of the remaining troops across to Gaul to drive them out.

In AD 408 a party of Anglo-Saxon raiders landed in Britannia. The Roman army had gone, but the Britons armed themselves and defeated the invaders. The Britons realised that they could not rely on the Romans any longer, and in AD 409 their leaders declared that Britannia was no longer part of the Roman Empire. Roman rule in Britain was at an end.

# Further work

## Time chart

Make a time chart to cover the four centuries of Roman rule in Britannia, from AD 43 to AD 407.

1 Begin your chart by copying this information:

ROMAN RULE IN BRITAIN

| Era | Date | Century | Important event |
| --- | --- | --- | --- |
| AD | 43 | I | Claudius orders his troops to invade Britannia |

2 Choose three important events from each century and add them to your chart.

3 Write a paragraph of two or three sentences about *one* of these events, showing why *you* think it was important.

## Writing: the empire and rebellions

1 (a) Name two countries besides Britannia that were part of the Roman Empire.

(b) Name one country besides Britannia where there was a rebellion against the Romans.

2 (a) Name the British queen who rebelled in AD 60.

(b) Why did she rebel against the Romans?

3 Explain in your own words:
(a) the difference between an empire and a kingdom;
(b) what a rebellion is.

## Making an exhibition
An exhibition is meant to attract attention. Make your work clear and bold.
1 Design a poster for an exhibition on 'Life and Work in Roman Britain'. Your poster should give some idea of what is on show; for example you might draw a mosaic pavement.
2 (a) Divide a double page or large sheet of paper into four sections.
(b) Write one of the following headings in each section:

Roman Britain          The countryside
Town life              The Roman army

(c) Choose a suitable picture or diagram for each section. Write not more than two or three sentences about it.
3 (a) Divide into groups of four. Within your group, choose one each of these topics:

Towns and town life    Country life
Soldiers and forts     Roads and travel

(b) Look through the section on Roman Britain in this book and choose a picture of something that was once used by a Roman, and that has been dug up, to illustrate your topic.
Draw a picture and write a sentence under it stating (i) what archaeological find is shown in your drawing; (ii) when and where it was found.
(c) Mount all four pieces of work from your group on one large piece of paper. Write a suitable heading. Display your work.

## Proving your point: how the Romans changed Britain
1 Write out these sentences, filling in the spaces. (The first sentence has been completed for you.)

They made the Britons submit to Roman rule, for example they showed no mercy to Boudica's rebels.
They built towns, for example _____
They made good roads for soldiers and traders to travel along, for example _____
They imported luxury goods into Britannia, for example _____

2 (a) Write a list of four points that you might include in a paragraph on one of the following statements:
Roman roads were well made.
Londinium was a great city.
The Roman army was an efficient fighting force.
(b) Write the paragraph, turning your points into interesting sentences.
3 By the time the Roman army was recalled to Italy the people in some parts of Britannia followed a Roman way of life. In other parts of the country, the Britons kept to their old ways.
(a) Copy the outline map of the British Isles which is facing page 1 of this book. Then write these names on your map in the correct places:

Scotland   Wales
Southern Britain   Ireland

(b) Compare your map with the maps on pages 12 and 26; then rewrite the list below. Begin with the region that you think was the most Romanised and end with the one that you think was the least Romanised:

Scotland
Wales
Southern Britain
Ireland

(c) Write a paragraph of four or five sentences, explaining why you have chosen the places that you have put first and last on your list.
(d) Explain what 'Romanised' means.

## Quizzes
1 *True or false?*
Julius Caesar conquered the whole of Britannia.
Roman women wore make-up.
The Romans had central heating in their houses.
2 *Find the odd one out*

Calleva   Housesteads   Londinium
Verulamium
Julius Caesar   Claudius   Hadrian
Tacitus
Suetonius   Boudica   Agricola
Antonius

3 Make up your own 'True or false?' or 'Odd one out' quiz.

# 2 Saxons, Celts and Monks from Rome

## Bede, a famous Englishman

### Bede translates the Bible

In the spring of AD 735 an old man and a boy sat at work in a small room in the monastery of Jarrow in Northumbria. The man, whose name was Bede, had in front of him a copy of the Gospel according to St John. It was handwritten in Latin on **parchment**. Every letter was carefully formed, and the capital letters at the beginnings of chapters were beautifully ornamented with coloured drawings of plants and animals.

Bede was studying the Gospel with great care. He read a few words to himself and then sat for several moments in silence, thinking hard. At last he turned to the boy, Wilbert, and spoke a few words in Anglo-Saxon. Wilbert wrote them down with his grey goose **quill**.

Together they were making a translation of St John's Gospel into Anglo-Saxon to be read in church to the people of Northumbria, most of whom knew no Latin.

### Bede's great learning

The work took many hours. Bede was ill. He was often weak and breathless, and found it difficult to concentrate for long. He also had many visitors to distract him. Most of them were other monks who crowded into his cell to see how he was and to ask for advice and information, for Bede was a very learned man.

▲ This detailed decoration of the first page of St Matthew's gospel must have taken many hours of patient work. It was all done by a monk on Lindisfarne in about 700

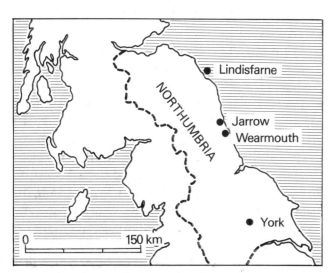

▲ Northumbria in the time of Bede

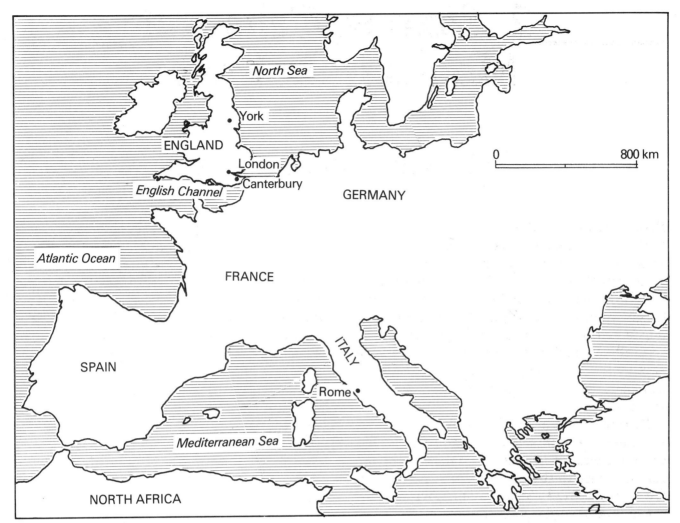

Map labels: North Sea, York, ENGLAND, London, Canterbury, English Channel, GERMANY, Atlantic Ocean, FRANCE, SPAIN, ITALY, Rome, Mediterranean Sea, NORTH AFRICA

0    800 km

▲ Nothelm visited Canterbury because it was the headquarters of the Church in England. He went to Rome because it was the headquarters of the Church in western Europe

He had read all the books in the library of the monastery at Jarrow. Visitors to the monastery had told him of other, larger libraries. The nearest was at York. Bede had made several visits there to consult books which were not in the library at Jarrow.

He had also heard stories of libraries in London, Canterbury and Rome. He had never visited these towns himself, but he had become friendly with a priest named Nothelm who travelled all over England, France and Italy on church business. Bede used to ask Nothelm to visit these faraway libraries and bring him copies of the documents he wanted to see.

## The books Bede wrote

Bede used the information he got to write books. Most of them were religious works, explaining difficult parts of the Bible, but he had also written a history of the English Church and a book on natural history. He had written all his books in Latin, so that they could be read and understood all over Europe. 'I have,' he wrote, 'worked honestly to pass on whatever I could find out.'

Some of the monks at Jarrow had made copies of Bede's books and sent them to libraries as far away as Spain, Germany and Italy. So although Bede had spent his whole life since he was twelve as a monk at Jarrow, his name was known all over western Europe.

When the monks of Jarrow came to see Bede they found him pale and gasping for breath in his cell. He welcomed them all, and tried his best to answer their questions. 'Learn quickly,' he said, 'I do not know how long I can go on, for God may call me in a short while.' And whenever he and Wilbert were alone, he dictated a few more words of the Gospel.

▲ A monk working in Northumbria at about the time when Bede was alive drew this picture of a scribe at work. The scribe's pen was made out of a wing feather from a large bird. The scribe had to harden the feather and cut it to shape

▲ The Saxon church at Bradford-on-Avon, Wiltshire, was once part of a Saxon monastery built in about 700

## Bede grows weaker

The days passed and Bede grew weaker. On 25 May he started work at dawn, and then talked to the other monks until they went away to a church service at about 9 a.m.

When Wilbert and Bede were left alone Wilbert said, 'There is still one chapter missing in the book you have been dictating, but it seems hard that I should bother you.' Bede was weak and very tired.

Bede roused himself. 'It is no trouble,' he said, 'take your pen, sharpen it, and write quickly.'

Wilbert did as he was told, and they worked together until about 2.30 p.m., when Bede said he would like to speak to some of the other monks. 'I have a few articles of value in my casket such as pepper, linen and incense,' he said, 'and I would like to distribute them as presents.' Cuthwin, a monk who was close at hand, went and called the others in.

## The death of Bede

The monks entered, and Bede spoke a few words to each of them, telling them that he had not much longer to live, and asking them to pray for him. They all stayed together until evening, talking and praying.

Then, when the monks had left, Wilbert, his mind still on his work, said, 'Dear master, there is one sentence still unfinished.'

'Very well,' said Bede, 'write this down,' and he dictated a few words.

Wilbert wrote, and then looked up. 'Now it is finished,' he said.

'It is finished indeed,' said Bede. Wilbert helped him down to the floor of his cell to pray. And there he died.

Bede's body was buried in the abbey church at Jarrow, but in about 1020 his bones were taken to Durham, where they still lie in a tomb at the west end of the cathedral.

# Studying the story

## How do we know?

### Cuthwin's letter

Soon after Bede died, a letter came for Cuthwin. It was from Cuthbert, a school friend who was now Abbot of the monastery at Wearmouth.

Cuthbert had written to say how sorry he was to hear that their old teacher had died. He asked Cuthwin to let him know what had happened.

Cuthwin wrote a long letter in reply. In it he described some of the things that Bede had said and done during the last days of his life.

1 Cuthwin saw Bede on the day he died. What are we told in the story that shows this?

2 We are given the words of a conversation between Bede and Wilbert. Did Cuthwin hear these words for himself, or were they reported to him? Give reasons for your answer.

3 What reasons (a) would Cuthbert have (b) do we have, for believing Cuthwin's account?

### Bede's books

Bede's books were in great demand. Orders for them came from all over Europe to Jarrow and Wearmouth.

Bede was the first Englishman to measure time from the birth of Jesus. In his famous *History of the English Church and People*, he tells the story of Britain from 60 BC to AD 731. He describes how, after the Roman legions left Britain in AD 407, the British Isles were invaded by heathen Anglo-Saxon tribesmen from Germany. They called the land they conquered 'England', and they were themselves often called the 'English'.

In AD 597 the Romans came again to these islands. This time it was not a great army that landed in Kent but a small group of monks. They came from the headquarters of the Catholic Church in Rome and were sent by Pope Gregory. The monks persuaded many Englishmen to become Christians. The Britons, who still held land in Cornwall, Wales and Ireland, had their own Christian Church. They hated the English and did not trust the Romans but at last they, too, agreed to join the Catholic Church. By uniting in one faith under the leadership of the Pope, these old enemies gradually grew closer together.

Bede thought it was important to tell this story well and he collected his information carefully. He listened to old stories told by the Anglo-Saxons of Northumbria and read books by Roman, Saxon and British writers. He even sent Nothelm as far as Rome to check facts.

Today, we still read his *History* to find out about the invaders who gave England its name and the Britons who struggled to hold on to their land and their own way of life.

1 Give an example of (a) written information, (b) spoken information that Bede used.

2 Why, as an honest historian, did he read books by Romans, Saxons and Britons?

3 How did he verify his information?

## Understanding what happened

1 (a) Which book was Bede translating?
(b) Why did he find it difficult to work?
(c) Who helped him finish his work?
(d) Do you think that the monk was right to encourage Bede to finish his work? Give reasons for your answer.

2 (a) Which libraries had Bede studied in?
(b) Which libraries had he heard about, but not visited?
(c) Which people made copies of Bede's books for libraries abroad?
(d) Why were there so few libraries when Bede was alive?

3 (a) Why did Bede have to translate Christian books into Anglo-Saxon?
(b) In which language did Bede write most of his books? What was the reason?
(c) What are we told in the story that shows us that Bede was a good Christian and a great scholar?

# Further work

## Copying and listening

1 (a) Turn to page 30. In your clearest writing copy from 'In the spring of AD 735' as far as 'thinking hard'.
(b) Decorate the first 'I' and draw some plants and animals.
(c) You have written about 100 words. St John's Gospel is about 18,000 words long. Would you need days, weeks or months to copy and ornament it?

2 (Work in pairs) Compare the sentence below with the first sentence on page 30:
'In the spring of AD 753 an old man and a boy sat at work in a small monastery at Jarrow.' The copier has made some careless mistakes.
(a) Together, find the mistakes.
(b) Separately, choose three sentences each from pages 30 to 32. Copy one sentence accurately, but make a deliberate mistake in the other two. Give the number of the page where you found each sentence.
(c) Exchange your work with your partner and see who can be the first to find the deliberate mistakes.

3 On page 44 you will find the parable of the sparrow.
(a) As a class, choose someone who can read well to read the story to you.
(b) Listen carefully to the reading.
(c) In pairs, take it in turns to retell the story to your partner. Give each other a grade A, B or C for accuracy.

## Writing

1 Imagine that you are collecting information in order to write an account of life in Britain during the last week.
(a) Write a list of five important events that you might include and say how you found out about them (for example: First woman lands on Mars—TV News).
(b) Did you obtain most of your information by reading, hearing or seeing it?
(c) Explain how you might verify your information.

2 Write an account of the death of Bede as it might have been reported by a monk other than Cuthwin. Think carefully about what he would have seen for himself and what he would have learnt from others.

3 Write an obituary or report of Bede's death as it might have been written by one of his pupils. Say you are sorry he has died and explain why you think he was a good teacher. (Think of a teacher you like and respect, how this teacher treats you and how Bede taught and talked to his pupils.)

## Drawing

1 Draw a book cover for Bede's *History of the English Church and People*. Include an illustration in your design—perhaps the map of the Anglo-Saxon kingdoms on page 36.

2 (a) Draw a map of places visited by Nothelm (see page 31).
(b) Write 'L' over the places where we know there were libraries.
(c) Underline Rome and Canterbury and explain why they were important religious centres.

3 Draw six pictures to show the stages in writing a book in the eighth century. Include: visiting libraries near at hand, sending abroad for information, writing copies of the book and sending them to other monasteries.

## What do you think?

1 Why did a scribe need good eyesight?
2 How did the Anglo-Saxons learn about the past if they could not read or write?
3 List three people today who do the work that the monks once did—translating, writing and passing on knowledge.

## Using your school library

1 Find the History section. If the section has a classification number, what is it?
2 Find the Reference Section and look up 'Writing' in an encyclopedia.
3 The monks wrote on parchment with a sharpened quill, which they dipped in ink. What else have people in the past written on, and with what?

# The Anglo-Saxon kings

The Kingdom of Northumbria in which Bede lived stretched from the river Humber to the shores of the river Forth. It was the biggest and most powerful kingdom in Britain.

The kings of Northumbria were descended from some of the Anglo-Saxon chiefs who had crossed the sea from north Germany to settle in Britain after the Romans left in AD 407.

At first these chiefs, or kings as they were called, and their armies had to fight hard to defeat the Britons. Gradually they drove them further and further west. Many Britons were killed. Others were captured and made into slaves. Eventually the Anglo-Saxons conquered the whole of England. The Britons were left with Cornwall and Wales. Look at the map on page 36.

Once they had defeated the Britons, the Anglo-Saxon kings began to quarrel among themselves as to how the country should be divided up. Soon the Anglo-Saxon tribes were at war with one another. The stronger tribes overcame the weaker and took their land until eventually there were only six or seven kingdoms left. The most important of these were Northumbria, Mercia and Wessex.

## The kings of Northumbria

The kings of Northumbria were very successful warriors. For example, in AD 603 King Ethel-

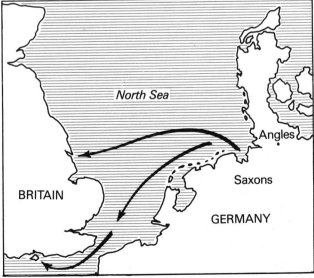

▲ The Angles and Saxons were two separate groups in Germany. The Angles gave their name to England

frith defeated the Scots at the battle of Degaston. Nobody knows where Degaston was, but the battle gave Northumbria control over all the border country as far north as Edinburgh. Then in AD 655, King Oswy of Northumbria defeated and killed King Penda of Mercia at a battle on the banks of the Humber. It was many years before a king of Mercia dared to attack Northumbria again.

## The life of a Northumbrian king

The king had a difficult job to do. He had to defend his kingdom. This meant that he was always on the move, because there was always trouble somewhere. While he was busy in the south, the Scots would invade from the north. When he moved north, the Welsh and the Mercians attacked in the south.

To make matters worse he could not always trust his own people. Even members of his family were quite likely to plot to get rid of him so that one of them could rule in his place. It was dangerous to be a king. In the middle of the seventh century, out of ten members of the Northumbrian royal family who lived to be adults, five were killed in battle and three were murdered. Only two members of the family died natural deaths.

The king had no settled home. He owned a number of palaces scattered about his kingdom and he travelled from one to another. On his journeys a standard-bearer walked or rode in front of him, carrying the royal standard. The king's family and advisers rode by his side, and they were surrounded by a large guard of armed fighting men. In time of war the king was joined by all the able-bodied men in the area who came, bringing their own weapons, to fight at his side.

## Life in a royal palace

We know a good deal about the appearance of royal palaces because a number of them have been excavated. The main building of the Northumbrian royal palace at Yeavering near Berwick-on-Tweed, was a wooden hall about 20 m long and 7 m wide, with doors at each end.

▼ Anglo-Saxon kingdoms. Anglo-Saxon kings often
invaded each other's territories, so the exact size and
shape of their kingdoms kept changing

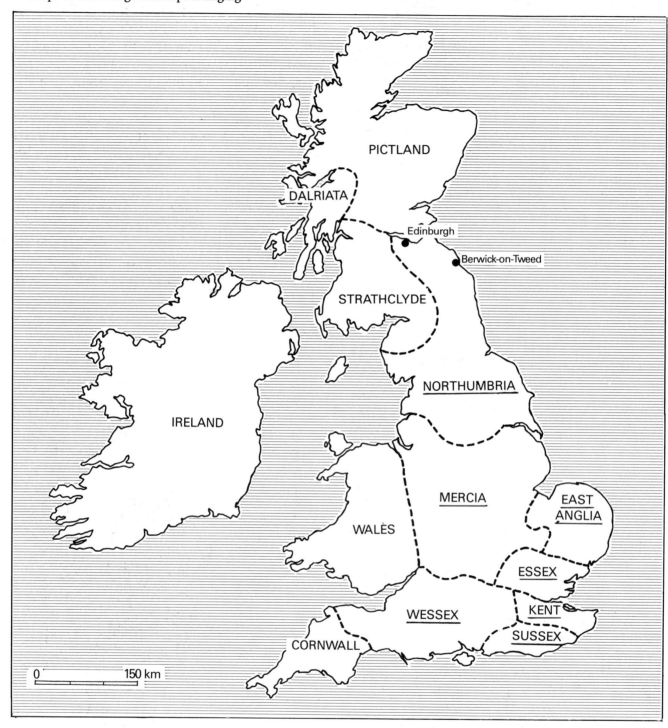

PICTLAND

DALRIATA

Edinburgh

Berwick-on-Tweed

STRATHCLYDE

NORTHUMBRIA

IRELAND

MERCIA

EAST
ANGLIA

WALES

ESSEX

KENT

WESSEX

SUSSEX

CORNWALL

0          150 km

In the evening there would be a feast attended by all the local landowners and the king's fighting men. There were slaves to serve the food and drink, and there was always plenty of beer, wine and **mead**. As they sat at table the king and his guests were entertained by a bard who sang songs of battle and adventure, accompanying himself on a small harp.

The king and his courtiers sat at a table set on the platform at one end of the hall. They ate from gold and silver plates and were richly dressed. The fighting men sat on benches at rough tables down the length of the hall.

At the end of the feast the king and his courtiers left the hall to sleep snugly in the nearby huts where beds had been prepared for them. The fighting men wrapped themselves in their cloaks and lay down to sleep around the fire in the hall.

▲ A drawing from an Anglo-Saxon manuscript showing a warrior carrying a wooden shield covered with leather, an iron sword and an ash spear tipped with iron. Many soldiers carried axes instead of swords

Near the hall there were a number of small wooden huts which were probably the royal family's private apartments.

At one end of the hall there was a raised platform where the king, his family and his advisers sat. In the middle of the building there was an open hearth. On this a fire blazed, but there was no chimney, and the smoke had to find its way out through a hole in the thatched roof.

The hall had many uses. During the day the king held court there. He received all the local landowners, listened to their problems, and settled any disputes between them. Then he gave them a report of what was happening in other parts of the kingdom.

▲ This drawing gives a good idea of the size of an Anglo-Saxon harp. The modern harp is much bigger, and has many more strings

▲ Archaeologists think that the royal palace at Cheddar in Somerset probably looked like this. One of the buildings near the main hall may have been a mill. Another was a bakehouse

▲ A Saxon nobleman

▲ A Saxon noblewoman

38

## Telling a story in the king's hall

After a good meal at the end of a long day, the king and his men liked a story with plenty of action. One story that the bards sang to them came from a long poem called *Beowulf*. It told how a monster called Grendel hated the King of Denmark because he had built himself a fine palace.

Each night, Grendel came from the cold, misty marshes where he lived and listened enviously outside the warm, firelit hall. From inside came the sound of harp music and the voice of the bard as he sang to the king and his companions.

The monster lurked in the darkness until the king and queen retired for the night and the warriors cleared the benches away, spread their bedding on the floor and went to sleep.

Then Grendel went into the hall and seized a warrior. He tore the man apart, drank the blood from his veins and gobbled up his body.

Imagine that you were one of the royal party at Yeavering. Describe:

How the king called for the bard to entertain everyone

How the bard sang the story of Grendel, using the notes of his harp to create a tense, eerie atmosphere

How you felt when it was time to go to bed (Think of an eerie story that you enjoyed while you were with other people but did not like so much when you were alone in the dark.)

### The king's government

Kings had a lot of expenses. They had to maintain their palaces, keep their families and pay their fighting men. They raised the money they needed to do this in various ways.

Kings owned a number of estates in different parts of their kingdoms. They let most of them out, and received rent for them. Sometimes the rents were paid in the form of produce such as cattle or corn. Sometimes the tenant had to provide his king with a few men to serve in the royal bodyguard. Sometimes he paid cash.

Kings also received taxes. All men who owned land of their own had to pay a tax to their king. Often it took the form of farm produce, but sometimes the landowners paid money. In either case they had to pay it in at the nearest royal palace.

Kings also got money from merchants, who had to pay taxes on the goods they imported and exported.

Some Anglo-Saxon kings became very rich. When a king of East Anglia died in the middle of the seventh century he was buried in a huge

▲ A solid gold belt buckle from Sutton Hoo (now in the British Museum in London). It is the finest piece of Anglo-Saxon jewellery ever found. It weighs about 400 grams and is beautifully decorated

▲ King Offa of Mercia, who ruled from 757 to 796, had these gold coins (18 mm diameter) made to the same pattern as Arab coins struck in the Middle East. But his were stamped with his Latin title, 'Offa Rex'

▲ An artist's idea of the Sutton Hoo ship

wooden ship 30 m long. His standard and a great deal of treasure, including a silver tray from Constantinople and some heavy gold ornaments, were buried with him at Sutton Hoo in Suffolk. In 1938 his grave was opened, and all its treasures are now on display in the British Museum.

### Anglo-Saxon law

In Anglo-Saxon times the law was very different from today. If a man was killed it was up to his family to catch the murderer and demand compensation. The value of a man's life was laid down by the law, and the price depended on how important he was. According to the laws of the Kingdom of Kent, written down towards the end of the seventh century, the killer of a prosperous landowner had to pay 300 **shillings**, while the murderer of a man who owned just enough land to feed his family had to pay 100 shillings. Some of the money went to the king to compensate him for losing a man who could have fought in his army or paid him taxes. The rest was kept by the murdered man's family.

If the family found the murderer and he had no money, his relatives had to pay. Once the money was paid the case was over, and the murderer went free. But if he and his family could not or would not pay, the family of the murdered man could kill him, or make him a slave.

Thieves and those who assaulted other people were also punished by fines. But money was scarce in Anglo-Saxon England, and few ordinary people could get hold of enough silver coinage to pay their penalty. So they were punished in other ways. Murderers were killed by hanging or beheading. Thieves were usually beaten, or branded with a red-hot iron. Other criminals had their hands cut off or their tongues torn out. Only people rich enough to pay the fines could be sure of avoiding punishment.

### Trials

If an accused man denied that he had committed a crime he tried to persuade all his family and friends to come forward and swear that he was innocent. Meanwhile his accusers were persuading people to swear that he was guilty.

Trials took place before a folk **moot,** which was a meeting of all free men in the area, with an official called the **reeve** in charge. The reeve was the king's representative, and it was his job to see that trials were properly conducted. Everything had to be done in the right order and using the right words. If a man forgot his words he could lose his case.

An accused man could also prove his innocence by submitting to trial by ordeal. He could choose one of three ordeals. In the ordeal by cold water he was plunged into the water. If the water accepted him and he sank he was innocent. If he floated he was guilty.

In the ordeal by hot water the accused man had to plunge his hand into boiling water and pick out a stone. In the ordeal by fire he had to carry a red-hot piece of iron for three steps. After these ordeals the man's hand was bandaged. Three days later the bandages were removed, and if his hand was healing without festering he was declared innocent.

# Anglo-Saxon gods and demons

We know very little about the beliefs of the Anglo-Saxons when they first came to Britain. We know the names of some of their gods such as Tuw, Woden, Thunor and Frigga, all of whom gave their names to days of the week. Place names sometimes tell where they were worshipped. Wednesbury means Woden's fort, Wensley is short for Woden's grove, while Thurstable means Thunor's pillar. There are many other such names.

We also know from their poems and stories that the Anglo-Saxons believed that deserts, lakes, marshes and mountains were inhabited by monsters such as fire-breathing dragons, demons, wicked goblins and sprites which one writer described as 'ferocious in appearance' and 'terrible in shape'.

## Charms and spells

To protect them from the power of these evil beings the Anglo-Saxons used all kinds of charms and spells. Some rich people wore rings with charms inscribed on them. A few of these have been found and the inscriptions seem to be just meaningless jumbles of letters. Poorer people carried their charms written down on parchment. They believed the charms could cure illness, make sure they had a safe journey, protect a house against thieves, and do all sorts of other things.

Charms were carried about, but spells had to be recited in a certain way, otherwise they would not work. For example, when bees were about to swarm their keeper was supposed to pick up some soil and throw it up with his right hand. He had to put his right foot on it when it landed and recite:

> I catch it under my foot. I have got it.
> Earth has power over all creatures
> And against envy and against forgetfulness
> And against the mighty tongue of men.

The purpose of this spell was to give the bee-keeper power over his bees. Then, when the bees swarmed, he had to throw some sand into the air where they were flying and recite:

> Settle, women of nature, sink to the ground.
> Do not fly wild to the wood.
> Be as keen to help me
> As men are to get food and land.

This spell was supposed to make the bees settle quickly so that the bee-keeper could easily collect them and put them into a new hive.

People used spells for all kinds of purposes, such as curing illness, increasing the fertility of the land or cursing enemies. Some wise men and women knew many spells and understood more about how they ought to be used than other people. These were witches and wizards, and they were feared.

▲ A man is attacked by elves. They have given him a terrible rash and shot arrows at him, and now they are stealing his clothes

▲ Runic writing, used by the Anglo-Saxons

## Trials, spells and charms

The diagram below shows a folk moot. Gurth has been accused of a crime and his family has brought him before the reeve to be tried. The family of Walda, the man who has been wronged, has come to accuse Gurth. A clerk sits near the reeve, waiting to record the events of the trial.

Gurth      Walda's family

1 (a) Draw the diagram and label: the reeve; Gurth's family; Walda.
(b) Write a sentence saying what crime Gurth may have been accused of.
(c) Describe what you think may happen to him as a result of his trial.

2 Study the picture of the man being attacked by elves on page 41. Edburga, the wise woman, is visited by Ingbert, who wants a charm to protect him on his travels. Write an account of their meeting.
*Things to write about:*
Edburga's description of the monsters and demons that Ingbert may meet
How Edburga warned Ingbert of what they might do to him
The type of charm Edburga gave Ingbert to protect him

3 The villagers know that if they cannot harvest a good crop of grain they will go hungry during the coming winter. Oswald, whose broken arm will not mend, and Hewald, whose crop of barley has mildew, go to see Elfric the wizard. Write an account of their meeting and its results.
*Things to write about:*
Oswald and Hewald tell Elfric about their troubles
Elfric gives each of them a spell and instructions to go with it
The two men cast their spells and, later, compare results

# Roman and Celtic missionaries in England

At the end of the sixth century Pope Gregory the Great was at the head of the Roman Catholic Church. He had heard of the heathen Anglo-Saxons living in Britain, and decided to send some missionaries to convert them to Christianity.

So in AD 596 a group of forty men, led by a monk named Augustine, left Rome to try to convert the Anglo-Saxons and set up churches all over England.

It seemed a huge task because England was split up into a number of different kingdoms, and most of the population lived in small, isolated villages. But Augustine knew that he did not need to go to every village. If he could meet the king and persuade him to become a Christian, the people would follow him.

Augustine and his followers landed in Kent in 597. Ethelbert, King of Kent, allowed him to set up his headquarters in the capital, Canterbury, and within a few months many of the king's subjects had been converted. Ethelbert himself did not become a Christian until later. Some of his family refused to accept the new faith. His

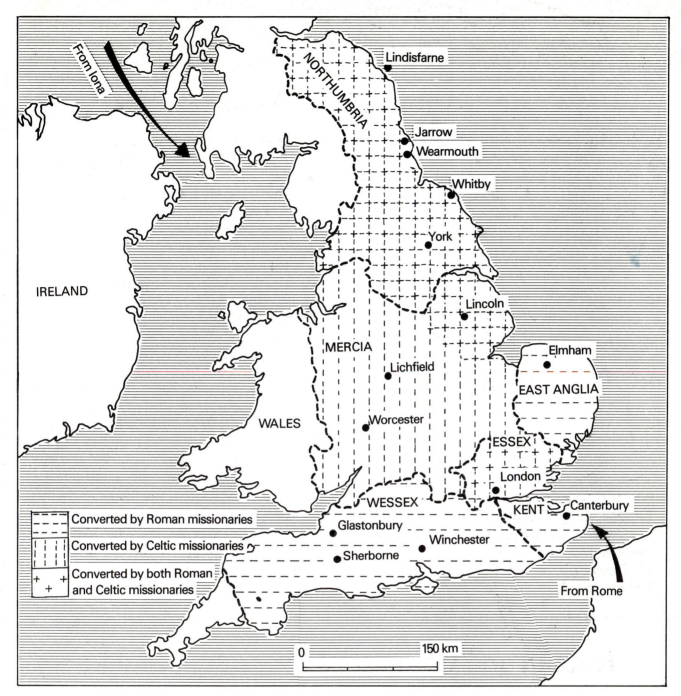

▲ Roman missionaries began work in the south-east and moved slowly north. Celtic missionaries landed in the north-west and moved south. Both Romans and Celts ended up in Northumbria

son, Eadbald, remained a heathen. But his daughter, Ethelberg, was baptised and took her new religion very seriously.

## Northumbria becomes Christian

In 625 Ethelberg left Kent. She travelled to Northumbria, where she married King Edwin, who was still a heathen. But Edwin had promised to allow Ethelberg to carry on with her own religion, and she took a priest named Paulinus with her to Northumbria.

As soon as he arrived in Northumbria, Paulinus began to try to persuade Edwin to become a Christian. Edwin hesitated. First he said he would agree if Ethelberg had a healthy child. A few months later she gave birth to a fine daughter. What was more, the birth was very easy. But Edwin went back on his word.

The West Saxons were attacking his southern border. He now promised that if he succeeded in defeating them he would become a Christian. Edwin's army defeated the West Saxons. But he still hesitated.

Finally he decided to call a meeting of all the most important men in his kingdom to discuss the new religion, and he promised that if they agreed he would become a Christian.

So Edwin called his advisers together and asked Paulinus to explain what Christianity meant. Paulinus did as he was asked. Bede tells us what happened next. In a famous passage in his *History of the English Church* he wrote that the leader of the king's priests liked the new religion, and said that they should hear more about it.

One of the king's advisers agreed, and went on: 'Your majesty, when we compare the present life of a man with that time of which we know nothing, it seems to me like the swift flight of a lone sparrow through the great hall where you sit in the winter months to dine with your thanes and counsellors. Inside there is a comforting fire to warm the room; outside the wintry storms of snow and rain are raging. This sparrow flies swiftly in through one door of the hall and out through another. While he is inside he is safe from the winter storms, but after a few moments of comfort he vanishes into the darkness from which he came. In the same way man appears on earth for a little while, but we know nothing of what went before this life or of what follows. Therefore if this new teaching can reveal any more certain knowledge, it seems only right we should follow it.'

The rest of the king's advisers agreed, and in 627 Edwin was baptised at York along with all the most important men in the kingdom.

### Celtic Christianity

Six years after Paulinus came to Northumbria some more Christian missionaries arrived. Their leader was a monk named Aidan. They set up a monastery on Holy Island, which they called Lindisfarne. From Lindisfarne they sent out preachers into the neighbouring parts of Northumbria.

These monks did not come from Canterbury. They were from Iona, an island to the west of Scotland, and their monastery had been founded in 565, more than thirty years before Augustine had landed in Kent.

The founder of the monastery on Iona was St Columba. He came from Ireland where the Celtic tribes had been converted in Roman times, and had remained Christians ever since.

Christians in Ireland lost touch with Rome over the years, and by the end of the seventh century some of their customs were different

▲ Bewcastle Cross, near Carlisle, was probably put up in about 700. Crosses were used to mark places of worship before churches were built. The masons who carved this cross covered it with complicated patterns, and carved a sundial on its south face

thought that all the clergy in his kingdom should be celebrating Easter on the same day, and should not waste time quarrelling over how monks ought to have their hair cut. He called a meeting of both sides so that he could hear what they had to say. He would then decide between them.

The two sides met at Whitby in 664. The Celtic case was put by Colman, a monk from Lindisfarne. He said he was following the teaching of Columba, who had founded the monastery on Iona.

Wilfrid, Abbot of Ripon, answered Colman. He said that the Roman customs were followed in Italy, France, Africa, Asia, Egypt and Greece. He went on: 'Indeed, the only people who are stupid enough to disagree with the whole world are these **Celts**.'

He also claimed that what the Pope said was more important than what Columba had taught because St Peter, the first Pope, had been given the power to decide who should be allowed into heaven, and this power had been handed on to every Pope ever since.

Oswy asked Colman if this was true, and Colman agreed that it was. Then Oswy smiled, and said that in that case he would side with Wilfrid and the Pope. 'Otherwise,' he remarked, 'when I come to the gates of heaven Peter, who holds the keys, may not be willing to open them.'

King Oswy's decision at the **Synod** of Whitby was very important. It helped the Pope to become head of the Church in all parts of England.

from those of the rest of the Church. For instance, Celtic monks shaved all the hair from the front half of their heads while other monks just shaved a round patch on top. The Celtic Christians also celebrated Easter on a different date and, more important, took no notice when representatives of the Pope in Rome told them to change their customs to fit in with the rest.

### The English join the Roman Church

These disagreements annoyed Oswy who became King of Northumbria in 642. He

## Monks and monasteries

Northumbria was famous for its monasteries. The best known were at Wearmouth, Jarrow, Whitby, Lindisfarne and Hexham. A monastery is the home of a number of monks, men who have vowed to spend their whole lives praying and working for the glory of God and the good of their fellow men.

Most monasteries were founded by rich men

who gave the monks land. The monks built their church and their living quarters on part of the land, and used the rest of it to grow crops for their food.

Some Celtic monasteries had both men and women living in them, but usually women who wished to spend their whole lives praying and working for God went to separate convents.

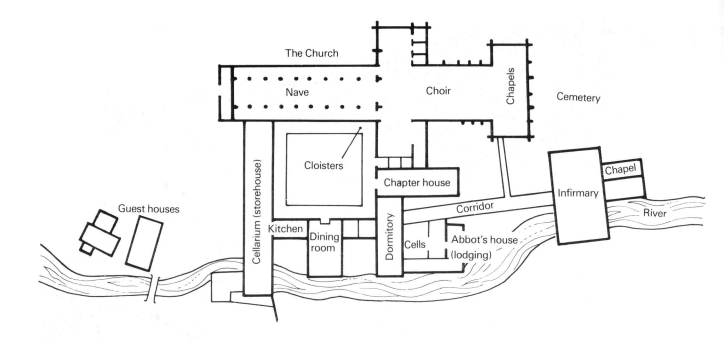

▲ Most monasteries were built on this plan. The
  cloisters were a sheltered walk where the monks
▼ could take exercise in bad weather

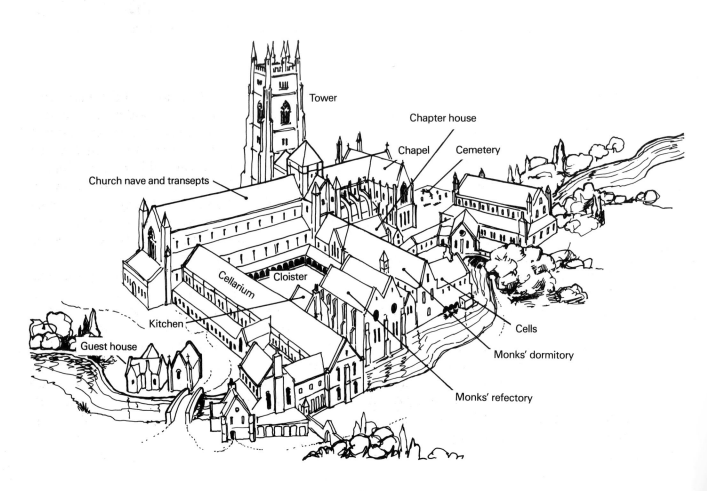

▲ This wall, which still stands, is part of the Anglo-Saxon monastery at Jarrow. The original windows, which were very small, have been partly blocked in

## The work of Benedict Biscop

The earliest Anglo-Saxon monasteries were built of wood, and there is now no trace of them. The Anglo-Saxon invaders did not know how to make mortar or cement, and so had no means of binding stones together to make a building.

But at the end of the seventh century Benedict Biscop, a rich Northumbrian nobleman, who had become a monk and had studied in France and Italy, founded the two monasteries at Wearmouth and Jarrow. Benedict decided that his monasteries should be much more splendid than any others in England, so he went to France and brought back masons who knew how to burn limestone to make quicklime. When this was mixed with sand and water it made a cement which dried hard and bound stones firmly together. Benedict ordered the masons to get to work and build his new monasteries in stone.

When the masons had finished the walls, carpenters came and put on a wooden roof, which was covered with a sheet of lead to make it waterproof. Then plasterers came and covered the insides of the walls with cream plaster. Finally French glaziers filled the windows with coloured glass. To go with the splendid buildings Benedict Biscop also provided books for the monks to study, and ceremonial robes for them to use in their services.

The founder of a monastery had a good deal of power over the monks who lived in it. He had the right to lay down the rules which the monks had to obey. Benedict Biscop decided that the monks at Jarrow and Wearmouth should live according to the rules laid down by St Benedict, a monk who had lived in Italy at the beginning of the sixth century.

## The life of a monk
*Summer timetable*

| Time | | Service |
|---|---|---|
| 1.30 | Get up | |
| 2.00 | | Nocturns |
| Daybreak | | Matins |
| 6.00 | | Prime |
| 8.00 | | Tierce |
| 11.30 | | Sext |
| 12.00 | Meal | |
| 14.30 | | Nones |
| 17.30 | Meal | |
| 18.00 | | Vespers |
| 20.00 | | Compline |
| 20.15 | Bedtime | |

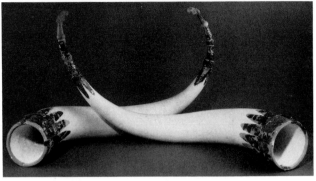

▲ Like most people at the time, Anglo-Saxon monks used animal horns as drinking cups. Sometimes they were richly decorated with carvings and had silver mounts fixed to them

The timetable shows that in summer the monks who followed the rule of St Benedict had a long day during which they had to attend eight services. In winter they got up at 2.30, went to bed at 18.30, and had only one meal a day.

The monks had to fit in five hours of work between the meals and the prayers. Some worked out of doors helping to produce food for the monastery. Others repaired the buildings. In some monasteries the monks were even expected to go out into the world to preach and convert heathens to Christianity.

Other monks were at work in the monastery. Some looked after travellers who stopped at the monasteries for food and lodging. The monks learnt a lot from them. Travelling merchants gave them news of what was going on in other parts of the country, and told them stories of other countries they had visited.

Some monks spent their time making handwritten copies of books to send to monasteries which did not have them. Others studied the Bible or taught children to read and write.

Life in a monastery seems hard, but in Anglo-Saxon times it was sometimes easier than life outside. Monks had enough to eat, and were sheltered from the weather by a lead roof and stone walls. They had books to study, music in their services, and stone carvings to admire. If they fell ill the other monks cared for them.

Some monks became famous. A few were made bishops, who each controlled the Church in a whole region. Others, like Bede, were well known as scholars. Some noblemen became monks, and so did members of the royal family, including several kings, who found the peaceful life of a monastery a welcome change from the hectic and dangerous time they had spent as kings.

Monasteries gradually grew richer. People asked the monks to pray for them, and in return gave land, money, jewels, statues, pictures and books. So monasteries gradually accumulated stores of valuable and beautiful things.

### Monasteries and learning
Monasteries were important centres of learning. They were the only places where there were any books, and monks were the only people who could teach children to read and write. Few girls and boys bothered to learn. Usually only those who were going to become nuns or monks themselves went along to the nearest convent or monastery to be taught.

Most pupils lived with the monks and had a hard life. A boy of twelve told a visitor: 'During the night when I heard the bell I got out of my bed, went to the church and sang Nocturns with the monks. Then we sang the service of All Saints and Matins, after that Prime and seven psalms, then Tierce and the mass of the day.

'After that we sang Sext, and ate, drank and slept. Then we got up and sang Nones. And now we are here in the schoolroom, ready to hear what you tell us.'

The boy ate meat, vegetables, eggs, fish, butter, bread and beans. He had ale or water to drink, but not wine. He slept in the same dormitory as the monks, and was beaten with a cane if he was late for services or made mistakes in his lessons.

Pupils spent most of their time learning to read, write and understand the Bible. But they also learned a good deal about the world around them. We know what Bede taught his pupils because we still have copies of a textbook he wrote, which was used in England and abroad.

## Bede's view of the world

Bede taught that the earth stood in the centre of the universe with all the stars, the sun and the moon revolving round it. The earth, said Bede, was round like a ball. It was divided into five zones. At the north and south there were areas of snow and ice. Sea captains had told him of the frozen sea which lay one day's sailing north of Iceland.

Around the middle of the earth there was a zone 'ever glowing with the flashing sun, ever scorched by his flames'. In between the heat of the equator and the frozen wastes at the two poles there were two gentle temperate zones where men could live.

Bede also taught that everything in the world was made of four elements—fire, water, earth and air. Hot springs proved that there was a great fire in the centre of the earth. Fire was produced by collision. If stones were banged together they made sparks. When clouds collided in the air they made lightning.

Just as there were four elements, there were four seasons, and man had in his body four humours or fluids which controlled his character. A man with a lot of blood was cheerful, lively and tender-hearted. A man with too much red bile was thin and irritable. Black bile made men solemn and cunning, while phlegm made them slow, sleepy and forgetful.

## Time and tide

Bede was very interested in the movement of the tides and the change of the seasons. He knew that at low water men could walk from the mainland to the monastery on Lindisfarne, while at high tide the path was covered with several metres of water. He also had to endure the endless dark nights of the northern winter, and enjoyed the long summer days. Scholars in the Mediterranean area, where there were no tides, and the length of the day did not alter much, had not given a great deal of thought to these matters.

Bede thought that in winter the sun moved south, so that the northern part of the globe saw less of it. He understood tides very well, and wrote the best description at the time of how and why they flowed as they did.

Philippus, a fifth-century scholar, had taught that movements of the tide happened at exactly the same time all over the world. Bede put him right. 'We who live by the far-flung shore of the British sea,' he wrote, 'know that when the sea has begun to flow at one point it is at the same time beginning to ebb at another.'

Bede pointed out that the tides moved in exact harmony with the moon. The Anglo-Saxons paid much more attention to the sun and the moon than we do today. Their only clocks were crude sundials, so when the sun did not shine they had no means of telling the time.

They used the moon to work out their calendar. From one full moon to the next was a month, and they counted twelve months to a year. This meant that their year lasted only 354 days, and they found that after a few years the months and the seasons were getting out of step, with the shortest day in February and the longest in August. To correct this they occasionally had a year with thirteen months. It was very confusing.

# Study

## Monks, missionaries and monasteries

### The coming of Christianity

1 Draw the map of Northumbria on page 30.
2 Write a complete sentence in answer to each of the questions below.
For example, you might begin your first sentence:

> The Roman and Celtic missionaries met in the Saxon kingdom of . . . . . .

(a) In which Saxon kingdom did the Roman and Celtic missionaries meet?
(b) Give two examples of religious customs that they disagreed about.
(c) Give the name and date of the synod where it was agreed that the Church in England should obey the Pope in Rome.

### Monasteries and the work of Benedict Biscop

1 Draw the plan of a monastery on page 46.
2 Write one or more complete sentences in answer to each of the questions below:
(a) What was a monastery?
(b) How did the monks use the land that was given to them by rich men?
(c) Benedict Biscop founded the monasteries at Jarrow and Wearmouth.

(i) How did he make his new monasteries more splendid than the earlier Saxon monasteries?
(ii) What did he give the monks to help them in their life of work and prayer?

### The life of a monk

1 Copy the timetable of a monk's day on page 48.
2 Write one or more complete sentences in answer to each of the questions below:
(a) How many services did a monk attend during the day?
(b) Give three examples of work done by the monks.
(c) Why did both rich and poor people find a monk's life attractive?

### Studying Bede's textbooks

Imagine that a monk in the eighth century is giving his class a geography test. His pupils have been studying Bede's textbooks. Give everyone ten minutes to make up two questions that the teacher might ask. Choose someone to be in charge of the test. Give him or her the questions, written on separate pieces of paper. Divide into two teams and give the test in the form of a quiz.

# Life in an Anglo-Saxon village

The Anglo-Saxons were skilled farmers. When they landed in Britain one of the first things they had to do was to find somewhere to sow their crops. Sometimes they took over land which had been cultivated in Roman times, but more often they cleared areas of woodland by burning down the trees and grubbing out their roots.

Once they had cleared some ground they divided it into long strips and shared them out among themselves. The richest and most important men got most. Slaves got none.

When they had ploughed and sowed one piece of ground, they cleared others until they had enough to grow food for them all. Even then they did not stop, for they knew that if they went on growing crops on the same land year after year the soil would gradually become less fertile.

So they cleared twice as much land as they needed and divided it into two huge fields. Each year they cultivated one of the fields and left the other without a crop to recover its fertility.

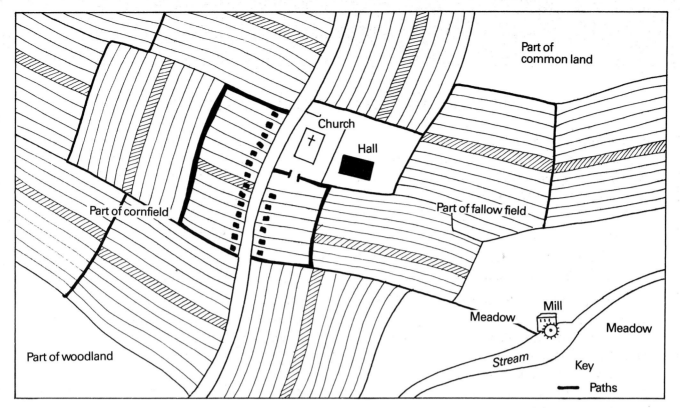

▲ Plan of a village. The shaded strips show the land
belonging to one man

## Ploughing, sowing and harvesting

Growing and gathering the crops was hard
work. First the farmer had to plough his land.
To do this he used a heavy wooden plough
which was dragged through the soil by a team of
four, six or even eight oxen.

A ploughman was supposed to be able to
plough an **acre** (nearly half a hectare) of land a
day. To do this he had to get up at dawn, drive
the oxen to the field and **yoke** them to the
plough. Then the team set to work. The man
was helped by a boy who jabbed the oxen with a
pointed stick to keep them moving. At the end
of the day the ploughman had to unyoke the
animals and give them food and water.

A sower followed the plough, walking along
scattering seeds on the ground. The farmers'
main crops were wheat, rye, oats and barley. In
addition they grew a small quantity of beans,
peas and lentils.

At harvest time the reapers had to work with
bent backs. They cut the corn with small sickles,
and carried it away to be stored under cover
until it was wanted.

▼ A team of four oxen, the boy with his goad, the
ploughman and the sower

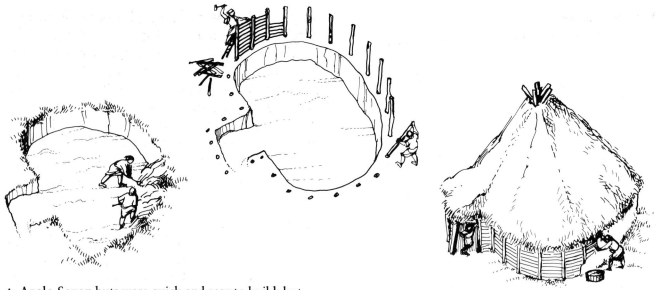

▲ Anglo-Saxon huts were quick and easy to build, but they did not last long

## Flocks, pasture and woodland

The Anglo-Saxons also kept sheep and cattle which grazed for most of the year on common pasture land. This surrounded the two **arable** fields. There were no hedges or fences. Shepherds and oxherds had to watch the animals to stop them wandering and prevent them being attacked by wolves or stolen. The shepherd's life was lonely, and when thieves were on the prowl it could be dangerous.

In the winter there was not enough food for all the cattle, so every autumn the farmers killed a number of them and salted the meat to eat during the winter. They kept the remaining animals alive through the cold weather by giving them hay and straw that had been cut in the summer.

Near the village there was usually a stretch of woodland. The forest was very important in the life of the farmers. Their pigs roamed through the trees rooting for food, while deep in the woods there were wild boars and deer to hunt. In addition the trees provided the timber which was used for building houses, making tools and for burning as fuel in the winter.

## Villages

Anglo-Saxon farmers lived in villages—clusters of buildings lying between the two arable fields. In some villages the buildings stood on each side of a long street. In others they were grouped round a village green where all the animals could be driven for protection if an enemy attacked.

Every village had a large hall where the **thane** lived. He owned most of the land in the village. Once the Anglo-Saxons became Christian, each village also had a church and a priest's house. The rest of the buildings were houses and sheds belonging to the farmers and their workers.

All the houses had gardens where people could grow a few vegetables, keep a hive of bees or rear a few hens and geese to provide them and their families with extra food.

At first all the buildings in the village were made of wood. They had a framework of large timbers with walls made of interlaced branches covered in mud. The roofs were thatched with straw, and had a hole in the middle to let the smoke out.

Most of the houses had no windows. If you closed the door to keep warm there was only the light of the fire or a spluttering candle made of dripping to see by.

## Village craftsmen

In most villages there was a smithy where the blacksmith worked at his forge and anvil making axe-heads, sickle-blades, spade-tips, fish-hooks, knife-blades and even needles. A skilled smith always had work to do, and must have used a large quantity of iron. This was made from iron ore dug from the ground and heated until it was white-hot in charcoal furnaces. These furnaces were always near to

▼ A smith at work

where the ore was found, and the iron had to be delivered to the smiths on horseback.

Many villages also had a tanner, who turned cattle skins into leather, and a cobbler, who made and repaired shoes. Most families produced their own cloth. The women made wool from their sheep into thread, and wove the thread into cloth on small looms.

Usually there was a river or stream near the village. The flow of water turned a mill wheel which provided the power for the miller to grind corn into flour. Villagers went to the stream with hooks, lines and nets to fish. They and their families usually ate everything they caught.

## Wandering pedlars

In most villages the people produced almost everything they needed. If they had to buy goods from outside, they relied on wandering pedlars who went from village to village buying and selling. Villagers living inland often had to buy salt. If they had large flocks of sheep they might offer wool or cloth in exchange. The pedlar would sell it in a village which had less pasture and so could only keep a few sheep.

Some villagers envied the pedlar as he travelled from village to village with his pack-horse. He saw more of the world than they did. But others thought of the lonely muddy tracks through the woods, of wolves and thieves, and they were glad to stay where they were.

## The farmers' diet

We cannot be sure what Anglo-Saxon farmers ate. They made some of their grain crops into bread, and brewed beer from some of the barley. They had a certain amount of meat, fish and honey, and they probably ate berries and seeds which they and their children gathered in the woods.

Some of their food must have been coarse and hard because it gradually ground their teeth flat. We know this from examining the skulls of skeletons found in Anglo-Saxon cemeteries.

We can also tell that many Anglo-Saxons died young and very few of them survived into old age. Many of the skeletons are those of children, and most of the others are of people who died before they reached the age of fifty.

## Games and amusements

The Anglo-Saxons had several games and amusements to help them pass the long winter evenings as they crowded round the fire. They played various board games, and gambled with dice made from animal bones.

When the fire sank low and the room grew dark they played word games. They tested each other with rhyming riddles. Some of these were written down, and have been translated. A monk at Jarrow asked what it was that could say:

> I am a simple thing, and am not at all wise.
> But clever men examine my foot prints.
> I now live on earth, but once wandered in heaven.
> Though I am all white, I leave black marks behind me.

The answer was a quill pen.

# Study

## Use your imagination

**The villagers and the pedlar**

1 Gurth, a pedlar, describes his life to a group of village children. Write an account of what he said to them.

*Things to write about:*
Gurth explains why the villagers need a pedlar to call on them
The kind of goods Gurth buys and sells
Carrying the goods from village to village
(Think of someone who has talked to you about his or her work and made it sound interesting.)

2 Wortha the pedlar is on his way to the village of Westerham. Write an account of how he arrives at the village, trades some of his goods and stays the night with Cuthman the tanner.

*Things to write about:*
Wortha comes out of the woods and walks along the village street
The villagers trade their produce for Wortha's wares
Cuthman's hut and the evening he and Wortha spent in it, talking and eating
(Think of someone you see from time to time whose visits you enjoy.)

3 Alda the ploughman says to Eadman the pedlar, 'I envy you. You do not have to stay in one place all your life as I do, working to support a family. You are free to go anywhere.' Write what Eadman might have said in reply.

*Things to write about:*
The enjoyable and interesting things about a pedlar's life
Times when a pedlar's life was hard
The advantages of being a villager
(Think of someone you envied until you found that his or her life was harder than you thought.)

## How can we tell?

How can we tell:
that the Anglo-Saxons ate some food that was coarse and hard,
that many Anglo-Saxons died young,
that the Anglo-Saxons buried their dead?

**Living in Anglo-Saxon England**
Life in Anglo-Saxon England slowly became less dangerous. Over much of the country there were many years of peace, and farmers could work in their fields knowing that they would not suddenly be called out in order to fight for their king.

The masons who had built the monasteries at Wearmouth and Jarrow taught their skills to others who built stone churches in many villages. The villagers knew that the inside of these churches would be dry and sheltered from the wind in bad weather, and gathered there to talk and sing.

But in 793 raiders from the sea landed on Lindisfarne and attacked the monastery. They dug up the altar, and carried off all the treasures of the church. They killed some of the monks and kidnapped others. The **Vikings** were on the move.

# Further work

## Time chart
Make a time chart to cover life in Britain from AD 400 to AD 800.

1 Begin by copying the information below:

| Era | Date | Century | Important event |
| --- | --- | --- | --- |
| AD | 407 | 5 | The Romans leave Britain |

2 Choose three important events from each century and add them to your chart.
3 Write a paragraph of two or three sentences about *one* of these events, showing why *you* think it was important.

## Writing: English invaders and British natives
'The English' is the name given to the groups of invaders who came to Britain from Germany in the fifth and sixth centuries.

1 (a) Into which parts of Britain were the native Britons driven?
(b) Which parts of Scotland did the Scottish tribes lose?
(c) Which part of the British Isles was not attacked and conquered by these invaders?
2 Explain in your own words: (a) what an invasion is, (b) who the natives of a country are.

## Readings and talks
1 (In pairs)
(a) Choose about ten lines to read on (i) a king's dangerous life, (ii) a monk's busy life.
(b) Prepare a passage each and read it to your partner.
(c) Draw an illustration to go with your talk.
2 (In groups of three)
(a) Take one of the following topics each and prepare a one-minute talk:
    The Four Elements
    The Four Humours
    Bede's idea of the world
(b) Give the talk to your group.
(c) Draw an illustration to go with your talk.
3 (In groups of four)
In an Anglo-Saxon poem called 'The Seafarer', a sailor tells how he left the safety of his village to travel and see more of the world. He describes his lonely life at sea, the cold driving rain and the cry of the sea birds. He has to suffer much hardship, but he has seen more than the people who stayed at home.
Take one of the following people each:
    the scribe  the warrior
    the smith  the farmer or his wife
Prepare and give a one-minute talk in which each person describes his or her life to the rest of the group.

## Proving your point
Look back through the section on Bede and the Anglo-Saxons. Find three examples to prove each of these points:
    Life was hard.
    Life was short.
    Christianity helped to make things better.

1 (a) Make a list of four important points that you might include in a paragraph to prove one of the following statements:
    Northumbrian kings never stayed long in one place.
    The Anglo-Saxons were skilled farmers.
    The Anglo-Saxons believed that words were powerful and that it was important to get them right.
(b) Write a paragraph, turning your list into interesting sentences.
2 (a) Write a list of three points on each of the following types of people, showing how each of them helped to make Northumbria a great kingdom: (i) kings, (ii) monks, (iii) farmers.
(b) Write three paragraphs, turning your lists into interesting sentences.

## Quizzes
1 *True or false?*
The Welsh and Irish were Christians before the English.
The English all obeyed the same king.
In the eighth century, Edinburgh was an English city.
2 *Odd one out*
Augustine Bede Oswy Cuthwin Cuthbert
Prime Sext Tierce Synod Nones
3 Make up your own 'True or false' or 'Odd one out' quiz.

# 3 The Vikings

## Egil's adventures in Kurland*

### The young Egil

According to the saga Egil Skalla Grimsson was a Viking warrior who lived in the tenth century. His family came from Norway, but his father, Skalla Grim, had quarrelled with Harald Finehair, King of Norway, and had gone with his family to live in Iceland.

Egil was dark and ugly. He had a quick temper, and was very strong. When he was seven or eight an older boy knocked him down in a quarrel over a ball. Egil went away and borrowed an axe from a friend. He returned, found the bully, and split open his skull with a single blow. When Egil's mother heard the story she was pleased. 'He is a real Viking,' she said.

### The voyage to Kurland

When Egil was a young man he went with his elder brother, Thorolf, on a voyage to the Baltic. They had a large ship with a crew of fine warriors, and everywhere they landed they robbed and killed.

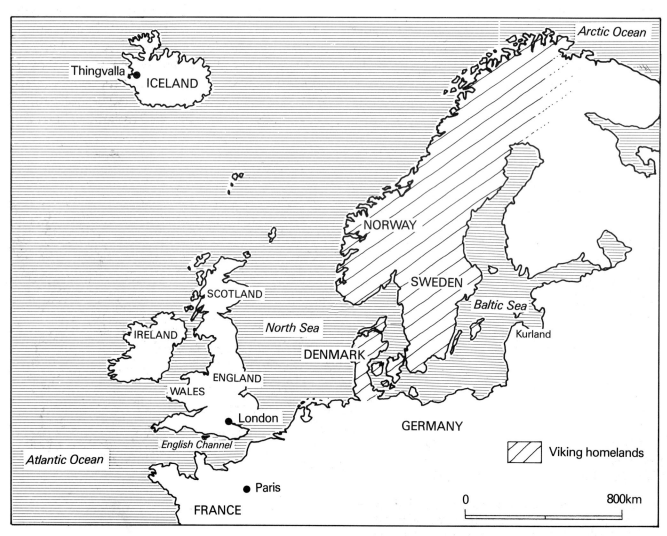

▲ The Viking homelands and neighbouring countries

* From *Egil's Saga*

At last they reached Kurland where they anchored at the mouth of a wide river whose banks were covered in forest. They split the crew into bands of twelve, and went ashore to explore.

## The house in the clearing

Egil and his band marched through the forest until they came to a clearing where there was a large wooden farmhouse with many small outbuildings. They quickly searched them, but found nobody. The inhabitants had run away leaving their belongings behind. So Egil and his men helped themselves, and staggered out of the house loaded down with clothes, food and drink.

## Egil is captured

Suddenly they stopped. For there, between them and the wood, stood a large number of armed Kurlanders. When they saw that there were only thirteen Vikings the Kurlanders came towards them, their swords and spears at the ready. Egil and his men dropped their booty and tried to fight off the Kurlanders with their swords and axes. But they were driven into a corner, and eventually they were all disarmed and captured.

By this time it was getting dark, and the Kurlanders decided to keep the Vikings prisoner until the next day, when they would torture and kill them. So they tied them up and locked them into a dark outhouse. Egil, who was stronger than the others, was tied to a stake driven deep into the ground.

## Egil escapes

As soon as the door closed, Egil began to rock the stake until it was loose in the ground. At last it fell over, and Egil was able to slide along until he was clear of it. Then he used his teeth to undo the ropes which bound his hands. He could now untie his feet and free his companions.

Once they were free they felt their way round the walls of the room. They found that three of the walls were made of solid timber. But the fourth was only a thin partition. They easily broke through it, and found themselves in another room. Beneath them they heard voices. They felt round and discovered a trap-door in the floor. They opened it and there in a cellar they found three Danes who had been captured and made to work on the Kurlanders' farm.

▲ The main farmhouse contained the dining hall. Here all the people who worked on the farm had to eat their meals. The smaller buildings were bedrooms, cookhouses, stores and stables

◀ This chest may have once contained the bones of a saint. Raiding Vikings stole it from an Irish monastery and took it back to Norway. When Egil opened the one he took, he found that it was full of silver

### Egil rescues the Danish slaves

Egil took the ropes which had been used to bind him and his men, lowered them into the cellar, and hauled the three men out.

The oldest of the three, Aki, knew the layout of the farm. He showed Egil a weak place in the wall of the room where they were, and they all broke out into the fresh night air. In the farmhouse lights were blazing, and there were sounds of laughter and singing. The Kurlanders were having a feast.

'If you want weapons,' said Aki, 'they will be in the farmer's bedroom', and he led them to a hut with an outside staircase leading to an upper room where two servants were busy preparing the farmer's bed. Egil crept up the stairs, and while the servants' backs were turned he tiptoed into the room, picked up an axe and killed them both.

### Egil robs the farmer's strong-room

The other Vikings followed Egil into the room and took swords, shields and axes. Then they noticed a trap-door in the floor. They opened it, took lights and went down. It was the farmer's strong-room, full of silver and other fine things. Egil picked up a locked treasure chest and tucked it under his arm. His companions all took as much as they could carry. Then they made their way back into the bedchamber, down the stairs, and stole away into the woods.

They had not gone far when Egil suddenly stopped. 'What we have done is wrong and wicked,' he said. 'We have robbed the farmer without letting him know what we were doing. We must go back and tell him, for no Viking ever robs a man behind his back.'

His companions disagreed. They wanted to press on to the ship. So Egil put down his treasure chest and went back alone.

### Egil kills the Kurland farmers

The feast was still going on. In a small hut by the side of the house Egil found the log fire which the cooks used to prepare the food. He grabbed the end of one of the logs and pulled it from the fire. He carried it to the house and pushed the burning end into the thatch of the roof. It caught fire.

Soon the house was full of flames and smoke. Some of the men inside collapsed, coughing and gasping. Others struggled to the door where Egil was waiting with his axe. As they stumbled out he killed them one by one. When they were all dead he made his way back to his men, picked up his treasure chest, and went back to the ship. In the morning they set sail, looking for other places to plunder.

### Egil grows old

Egil lived until he was over eighty. As well as being a warrior he was a poet and doctor. He also knew how to put a curse on people. Everyone feared and respected him.

# Studying the story

## How do we know?

### Egil's saga

The Vikings of Egil's time did not value books and book learning. Instead, they admired a man with enough quick wits and cunning to lead a successful raid or tell a good story. The heroes in the stories had to endure hardship bravely, for a Viking's life was hard and dangerous.

Winters are long in Iceland. To pass the time, families sat around the hearth, listening to the storyteller. The stories changed and grew, until real people, ships and seas became part of a legend in which fact and fiction were mixed up.

Egil had been dead for over two hundred years when his story was first written down. Like many of the sagas, it is not an accurate account of his adventures. Instead, it tells us what men by that time *thought* had happened, and what they liked to believe about their sea-faring forefathers.

1 (a) What did Egil do when young that made his mother say he was 'a real Viking'?
  (b) Give an example of his courage when he grew up.
2 (a) Given an example to show that Egil was quick-witted.
  (b) Which did he think was worse, to rob the farmer, or to rob him behind his back?
  (c) Could Egil do anything well, apart from fighting?
3 Storytellers often exaggerate to make their story more satisfying. Does any part of the story of Egil seem exaggerated to you? Give reasons for your answers.

### The coin hoard

If the Kurlanders had not captured Egil, he would have missed the most valuable loot of all—the farmer's coin hoard.

Any man wealthy enough to own a hoard of silver guarded it well. With the coins he could buy more land. Sometimes he might buy silk cloth or golden ornaments from abroad. These goods added a little comfort and even luxury to his hard life.

If he thought his home would be attacked, he might bury his hoard, hoping to dig it up again when the danger had passed. If he did not return, the hoard might lie undiscovered for centuries. In 1952, a hoard was found under a large stone at Gandarve in Sweden. It was made up of these coins:

15 Arab   432 German  9 Danish
 2 Irish  212 English  2 Bohemian
                          (Czech)
221 Viking copies of English coins

Some hoards must still be lying, undiscovered, where they were buried hundreds of years ago.

1 (a) Which room did Egil have to go through to reach the farmer's strong-room?
  (b) Describe the hut the strong-room was in, showing how the farmer had tried to guard his treasure.
2 Study the picture of the chest on page 58. Sometimes, coins have been found, but the purses they were buried in have disappeared. Why do you think the purses have vanished, while this chest has survived?
3 Study the details of the Gandarve coin hoard.
  (a) How many countries did the coins come from?
  (b) What do you think mattered most to the Vikings, where the coins came from or what they were made of? Give reasons.

→

# Understanding what happened

1 *People and countries*
   (a) Which country did Egil's family live in before they went to Iceland?
   (b) Which sea did Egil and his men sail to when they raided Kurland?
   (c) Which country did the Kurlanders' slaves come from?

2 *The farm*
   (a) What were the buildings made of?
   (b) Give two examples to show how Aki's knowledge of the layout of the farm and its contents helped the prisoners to escape.

   (c) What was the hut by the side of the house used for, and why may it have been built a little way from the house?

3 *The raid*
   (a) Why did Egil need raiders who were both good sailors and powerful warriors?
   (b) How did Egil divide his crew when they reached land and why may he have done this?
   (c) Why was Egil able to kill so many Kurlanders, even though his crew had left him to fight alone?

# Further work

## Writing

1 In the saga the following items may be based on fact:
   (a) the voyage overseas
   (b) the description of the farm buildings
   (c) the hidden coin hoard
   Write the story of Grimm, an imaginary Viking hero, who led a raid overseas. Include the items listed above in your story.

2 Imagine that you are helping to clear some land. You move a boulder and find a coin hoard. Describe:
   > How you found the hoard
   > How you opened the casket and found the coins
   > What the curator at the museum told you about them

   (Think of something interesting that you found hidden where you least expected it.)

3 Imagine that Egil's raid really took place and a Kurlander lived to tell his tale. Describe the Kurlander's feelings about 'a true Viking' who
   > led an attack on his farm;
   > stole his goods and burnt his home;
   > killed his family.

   (Think of something that other people have done to you, that they thought was clever, but you found hurtful.)

## Mime

In groups of five or six, prepare a mime telling the story of Egil's adventures. Each group takes one of the following episodes to prepare and perform to the rest of the class:

1 Egil kills the bully
2 Egil and his men land, loot the farm and are captured
3 Egil escapes and frees his companions and the Danes
4 They kill the farmer's servants and steal the treasure
5 Egil burns the hall, kills the Kurlanders and sails away

## Drawing

1 (a) Draw the map on page 56.
2 Study the picture of the chest stolen from an Irish monastery on page 58.
   Draw a picture of Egil opening the treasure chest.
3 Draw a picture of something Egil did in the story that showed he was 'a true Viking'.

## What do you think?

Why did the peaceful Icelanders of the twelfth century enjoy the stories about their warlike forefathers? If Egil's saga is not real history, why do historians study it?

# Life in the Viking homelands

### The homelands

The Vikings, or Northmen, lived in Norway, Sweden and Denmark. Norway is a wet, mountainous country with short summers and long winters. There is very little land suitable for farming, but in Viking times there were vast forests, and the North Sea teemed with fish.

Sweden is much less mountainous, and has many lakes. The climate is cold and dry, but the ground is easier to cultivate and suitable for growing oats, rye and barley.

Denmark is by far the smallest of the three countries. It has a mild, moist climate, and the land is easy to farm.

### Viking farmhouses

Most Vikings were farmers. In Norway and Sweden they lived in oblong, straw-thatched houses with wooden frames and walls made of wattle and daub. They often built a wall of stones and turf round the outside of the house to protect it from the cold winter winds. The house had no windows. It had a wooden door and a hole in the thatch to let out the smoke.

Most houses had two rooms, with a thin partition in between. The farmer, his wife and their children lived in one room, and his sheep and cattle spent the winter in the other. The heat from their bodies helped to keep the whole house warm.

Along the walls of the family room there was a low, wide, timber shelf. This was used as a seat during the day, and as a bed at night. In the middle of the floor there was a stone hearth, on which a fire burned day and night.

▲ This modern reconstruction of a Viking farmhouse shows how dark and uncomfortable they were. Smoke from the fire in the middle of the floor got into people's clothes, making them smell

▲ This chair was made by a Viking craftsman. It was found in 1903 in a burial ship at Oseberg in Norway

▲ The bowl of this lamp was filled with animal fat. It burnt with a very smoky flame and gave a poor light

## Cooking

Next to the fire there was a hollowed-out roasting pit. When the Vikings wanted to roast meat or fish they wrapped it in leaves or in a thin layer of clay, and put it into the pit. Then they surrounded it with stones which they had heated in the fire, and left it there until it was cooked.

They made stew by boiling meat or fish in a cooking pot made of iron or **soapstone**, which they hung over the fire. They ate from wooden dishes, plates and bowls.

Most families also had a small clay oven for baking bread. They heated the oven by burning a fire of twigs in it. When the oven was hot enough they raked out the ashes and put the bread in to cook.

The Vikings were famous for their skill in working and carving wood, and many farmhouses were furnished with sturdy wooden chairs. Some of these were decorated with intricate patterns carved into the wood.

Most farmhouses also contained a loom on which the women wove coarse woollen cloth, and a simple lamp for the winter evenings.

## Life in the Viking homelands

Study the map of the Viking homelands on page 56.

1 Which country was (a) wet and mountainous? (b) mild and moist? (c) cold and dry?
2 Which country was (a) easiest, (b) most difficult to farm?
3 Give two reasons why the people of Norway became skilled fishermen.

### What do you think?

Why was it difficult for most Northmen to become prosperous farmers?

### The Viking farmhouse

1 Read the description of Viking farmhouses on page 61. Then copy this outline plan of a Viking farmhouse.

```
                    Outer wall
       ┌─────────────────────────────────────┐
       │   ┌─────────────────────────────┐   │
Door   │   │ ☐  Hearth       │           │   │
       │   └─────────────────────────────┘   │
       └─────────────────────────────────────┘
```

Now add:
    the family's living quarters
    the animals' quarters
    the cooking pit
    the timber shelf

2 (a) Why did the house have (i) no windows? (ii) an outer wall of stone and turf?
(b) How did the animals help to keep the house warm?
(c) Give two reasons why the fire was always kept burning.

### What do you think?

1 Which was more important, to make sure that the house was warm and dry or to keep it smelling clean and fresh? Give reasons for your answer.
2 Study the pictures of the chair, lamp and loom on pages 62 and 64. Give an example to show how the Northmen used each of the following in their homes: (a) wood, (b) stones, (c) animal fat.
3 How were people able to survive in such a harsh climate?

▲ A Norse farmer

▲ A Norse woman

## Work and crops

The farmer and his family had to work hard. In many places, especially in the north of Norway and Sweden, the fields were too small to be ploughed, and the farmers had to break up the soil with iron-tipped poles or wooden spades. They fertilised the fields with animal manure which they carried from the house on a sledge. The work was very heavy. Some farmers had to do it all themselves with a little help from their families. Others had slaves to do the hardest work.

The farmers grew barley, rye, oats, peas and onions to feed themselves, but they had to spend most of the growing season looking for food for their animals. As soon as the grass began to show green on the low ground the farmers drove the cattle out to graze. Then, as the days got longer and warmer, the grass on the hills began to grow. The farmers drove the animals up onto the slopes and left them there for the summer. They were guarded by the farmers' children, who lived in a rough shelter, and spent their time milking the cattle and making cheese.

Meanwhile the grass on the lower pastures continued to grow, and the farmers cut it and dried it to make hay for the winter. In the north cattle had to be kept indoors for about 200 days a year, so each cow needed about 2½ tonnes of fodder to stay alive. The farmers searched everywhere for food. They even stripped leaves from some of the trees and dried them to feed to their animals in the winter.

In the autumn the cattle were brought down from the high pastures. The farmers worked out how much fodder they had and how many animals they could keep through the winter. They killed the rest. The autumn was also the time when they had to harvest and store their crops, and make sure that they had enough wood or peat to keep the fire going through the long winter.

The farmers' wives also worked hard. They ground the grain into meal and flour, baked bread, brewed beer and salted away the meat from the animals that had been slaughtered in the autumn.

## Winter work

In the winter there was less work to do on the farm. Many of the men spent their time making

▲ Simple looms like this one were used in Viking farmhouses. The weight of the stones at the bottom kept the vertical threads stretched taut

furniture or carving ornaments from wood or bone in the lamplight. Their wives and daughters spun thread on a **distaff**, or wove cloth on their loom.

In some parts of Denmark and southern Sweden where the winter was short and the soil good, the Vikings found it easy to make a living from farming. But in the north of Norway they could never grow enough food to survive, and they had to hunt deer, go fishing and scramble over rocky cliffs to catch birds and collect eggs in order to have enough food to eat.

## Viking towns

Some Vikings lived in towns. These were trading posts, and were nearly always situated on the coast. Ships brought cargoes of slaves, salt and iron and luxuries like gold, silver and silk. In the towns there were craftsmen who could make the iron into knives, arrow-heads and axes, and fashion the gold and silver into coins and jewellery. To pay for all these goods the farmers and trappers brought in fur, ropes made of animal hide, sheep, cattle and grain.

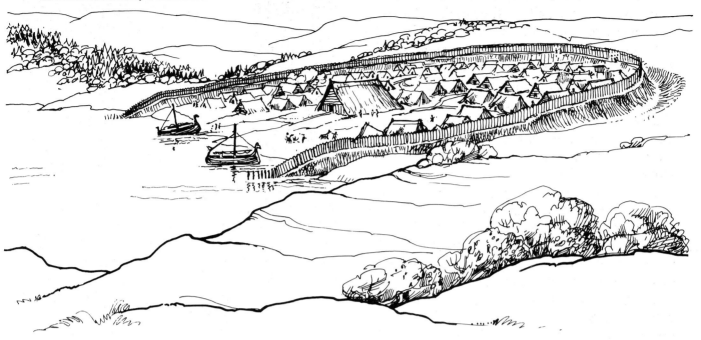

▼ Aros was built on very low ground. There were many marshes around it, which made it difficult to attack

## Town walls

Viking towns were small. They were always well defended. Aros, on the east coast of Denmark, had the sea on one side. On the other three sides there was a steep earth rampart faced with wood. The townsmen built a stout wooden fence on top of the rampart, and laid a wooden road behind it to enable their warriors to make their way quickly from one part of the ramparts to another.

## Houses

Most of the houses in the town were small square buildings known as pit dwellings. The floor of the house was about a metre below ground level, and on each side of the house the eaves of the thatched roof touched the ground. The walls were lined with logs of wood that were held in place by posts driven into the ground. These homes were windproof, but very damp. In the centre of the town stood the larger

▼ These buildings were very easy to heat, because they were small, and the thatch was thick. But they were very dark

and more comfortable houses of the rich merchants.

In Aros, as in other Viking towns, wooden buildings were packed very close together, with only narrow lanes between them. Fire was a constant danger, and in a strong wind the whole town could be destroyed in a few hours.

## The Thing

The Vikings had kings to rule them and lead them in battle, but they made all the most important decisions themselves. Every two weeks, at new moon and full moon, all free men who were fit to bear arms had the right to attend a meeting at which local disputes were heard and settled. The Vikings called these meetings 'Things'.

At a Thing meeting representatives from each side had the right to state their case. Then an official known as the lawman recited what the laws of the province, which he knew by heart, said on the subject. Finally all the men present gave their verdict. Everyone had a vote.

People often quarrelled at Thing meetings, but there were never any fights because it was a strict rule that nobody should be harmed at a meeting, or on their way to and from the Thing.

If the local Thing could not decide a case, it was sent to the provincial Thing, which was much more powerful. It could make new laws, and before a new king could take over his kingdom, he had to get the approval of all the provincial Things in the kingdom.

The most important men in the area attended meetings of the provincial Thing, and they spent a good deal of time discussing and criticising what the king was doing. The Vikings believed in luck, and if they decided that their king was unlucky, they would vote to get rid of him and elect another. If the other provincial Things agreed, the king was deposed. The ordinary free men did not often speak when the chieftains were talking about the king, but they banged their swords on their shields when they agreed with what was said.

Sometimes the king himself would come to meetings of a provincial Thing. When he did he had one vote, the same as everyone else. Nevertheless he could often get his own way. When the people saw him ride up on a fine horse

▲ The Viking Thing place on the Isle of Man. The King of Man stood on top of the mound. His nobles stood around him near the top. The ordinary people stood lower down

with gilt ornaments flashing on its harness, accompanied by a large band of armed men, they were impressed. And when he dismounted everyone could see his splendid clothes and his richly decorated sword and helmet. Few people at the Thing dared to criticise so rich and powerful a man to his face. So most of them agreed with whatever he said.

# Study

## The Thing

### Viking government

1 Choose the right word to fill the spaces in the sentences below:

province  Thing  locality  kingdom

Each Viking kingdom was ruled by a king. The _____ was divided into provinces and each _____ had a provincial Thing. The provinces were divided into localities and each _____ had a local _____.

2 (a) Which of these people could vote at a local Thing?

(i) Bjarni the lawgiver, (ii) Thorfinn, a strong, fit farmer, (iii) Aswald, son of Thorfinn, who had just returned from fighting overseas, (iv) Gudrun, Thorfinn's wife, (v) Caed, a slave.

(b) Why could the other people *not* vote?

(c) If the local Thing could not settle a quarrel, where was the case sent?

3 (a) Which powerful people attended the provincial Thing?

(b) Give three examples of their power over the king.

(c) The Vikings were impressed by power and riches. How could a cunning king impress the Thing and get his own way?

### Gods and the after-life

The Vikings believed in a number of gods. The most important was Thor who controlled the weather and made thunder with his hammer. Odin was the god of war and valour. He rode an eight-legged horse, and carried a pet raven on his shoulder. Frey was the god of crops and fertility.

▲ A carved slab showing Odin on his eight-legged horse

▶ A statuette of Thor, resting his hammer on his knees

The Vikings made up many stories about their gods. They imagined them feasting at their home at Valhalla, where all brave warriors would join them after death.

In order to win the favour of their gods the Vikings made sacrifices to them. They killed dogs, horses and even people, ate a little of the flesh and then hung the bodies on trees to rot.

The Vikings believed in life after death. They thought that a dead man or woman needed the same kind of food and equipment as when they were alive. So when they buried a rich man they put plenty of food into the grave with him, as well as clothes, ornaments and bowls. They killed horses and even servants, and buried them with their master to serve him in the after-life. The graves of the rich were well worth robbing, and thieves looted most of them, often only a few years after the funeral.

Life was cheap in Viking times. Fathers killed their newborn children if they were weak or deformed, and most Vikings believed that it was better to die young in a fight, trying to win treasure to share with friends, than to spend a long life at home avoiding danger.

# The Viking explorers

**The homelands fill up**

When a Viking died his eldest son took over his land. His younger sons had to leave home and make a living somewhere else. Until the middle of the eighth century they were able to find land in Norway, Sweden and Denmark, but by about 750 all the land had been taken. The Viking homelands were full.

Many younger sons listened to the stories of merchants who called at Viking ports, and heard them tell of rich lands across the sea where the climate was gentle and there was

▲ Viking ships on a raid

plenty of treasure. They could not resist the thought of all this wealth. So, like Thorolf and Egil in the story, they got together a crew, hired a ship and went off to explore.

### Viking sailors
The Vikings learnt to sail in the stormy waters of the Baltic and the North Sea. Even though the sea was often rough, it was easier and quicker to sail from one coastal village to another than to struggle on foot over the cliffs and mountains. So the Vikings used ships a lot, and were just as much at home on the water as they were on land. They were not afraid to sail in unknown seas and land on an uncharted coast.

### Viking ships
The Vikings had fine oak ships which were carefully shaped to slide quickly and easily

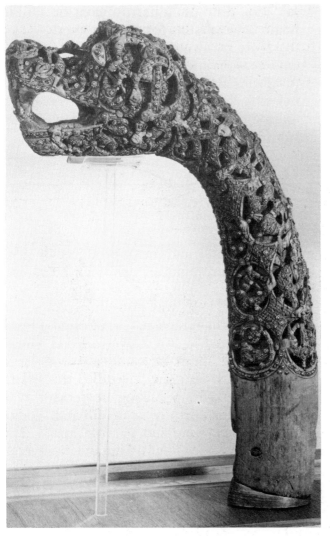

▲ Viking figureheads were often carved to look like dragons' heads

through the water. Each ship had a mast with a square sail, but when the wind dropped the crew lowered the sail and rowed the boat with long wooden oars. To keep the boat on course the helmsman used a steering oar lashed to one side near the stern.

The boat-builders took great care to make their ships strong and safe. They made the keel out of the trunk of a single oak tree so that it had no joints to weaken it. They fixed oak planks to the wooden frame with iron nails, and crammed animal hair mixed with tar into the gaps to make them watertight. When the ship was finished they decorated it with a carved wooden figurehead on the prow.

The ships varied in size. The smallest, up to about 12 m long, never went far from the shore, but the larger boats, which were up to 25 m long, could easily cross the open sea. Narrow boats were fastest, and were used by warriors. Wide boats were slower, but were better for carrying cargo and animals.

Viking ships could sail in very shallow water. This meant that their crews could land almost anywhere. They did not need to look for a harbour. Often they ran their ships straight up a sloping beach, and climbed out over the side.

The Vikings loved their ships and gave them names like Sea Horse and Keel Bird. They were right to be proud of them. In 1893 craftsmen built an exact copy of a Viking ship, and a crew sailed it across the Atlantic from Norway to Newfoundland.

### The Vikings sail westward
After about 800, large numbers of Vikings began to look for new lands to settle in. Raiders from Norway landed on the Shetland and Orkney islands and the Faeroes. Then they moved south to the Hebrides, the Isle of Man, Ireland and the west coast of England.

Once they had settled on the Faeroes it was not long before they discovered Iceland. One of the first settlers there was Egil's father, Skalla Grim. He was a skilled craftsman. He was a good smith, he could build boats, and he knew how to farm and fish. With the help of his family, his slaves and their wives he was able to build up a prosperous settlement.

# Study

## Viking ships

In 1881, a Viking ship was excavated at Gokstad in Norway. Here are its measurements:

| | |
|---|---|
| Length | 23.33 m |
| Width at widest point | 5.25 m |
| Height of mast | 12.00 m |

1 Measure the length of your classroom. Is it longer or shorter than the ship?
2 Measure the width of your classroom. Is it wider or narrower than the ship?
3 Who is the tallest person in your class? How many times taller was the mast of the ship?

Study the picture of a Viking ship on page 68.
1 (a) Draw the ship.
 (b) Label the sails and steerboard.
 (c) One Viking thought that his ship moved swiftly and gracefully over the water like a seabird skimming across the waves, so he called it *Keel Bird*. Make up a name for a ship that gives the same idea of speed and grace.
2 The Vikings thought of death as a voyage. They burnt the bodies of their dead chieftains and buried their ashes in ships like the ones found at Gokstad.

Imagine that a Viking leader has just died. Describe:
 His funeral ship
 The objects his followers put in the ship with his ashes
 How they praised his bravery and prayed to Odin to take him to Valhalla

3 Imagine that a Viking is planning to take his family from Bergen in Norway to Reykjavik in Iceland. He has a wife, four children and a slave and ten animals.
 (a) Would he use a narrow boat or a wide boat? Give reasons for your answer.
 (b) How many oars would he have needed? Give reasons for your answer.
 (c) From Bergen to Reykjavik is 900 sea miles. A Viking cargo boat could travel 150 miles a day. How long would it have taken from Bergen to Reykjavik?

### Greenland and America

Just after 900, a Viking living in Iceland was blown off course when sailing home from Norway. Far to the west he saw a huge unknown land, but he did not stop to explore it because he wanted to get back to his home in Iceland.

More than fifty years later a quarrelsome Norwegian, Eirik the Red, was sent into exile by the King of Norway. He went to live in Iceland, but was banished again. So he set sail in search of the new land to the west. He found it, landed and built himself a farm there. Then he returned to Iceland and tried to persuade other people to come and join him. To make the new country sound more attractive he called it Greenland.

In the end several families of settlers joined Eirik. They had a hard life. The summer was too short to grow grain, so they had to rely on the meat, butter, milk and cheese produced by their animals and on reindeer, fish, seal, bears and whales.

Eirik's son, Leif, was also an explorer. He sailed west from Greenland, and found a large country covered in forest. He called it Markland. Further south he came across a large island where vines grew. He called this island Vinland. In time a Viking settlement was founded on the north coast of Vinland. Today Vinland is Newfoundland, part of Canada. The Vikings had crossed the Atlantic and discovered America.

### Voyages from Denmark

Danish ships sailed further south than the Norwegians. A Danish army landed on the north coast of France to fight for the French king,

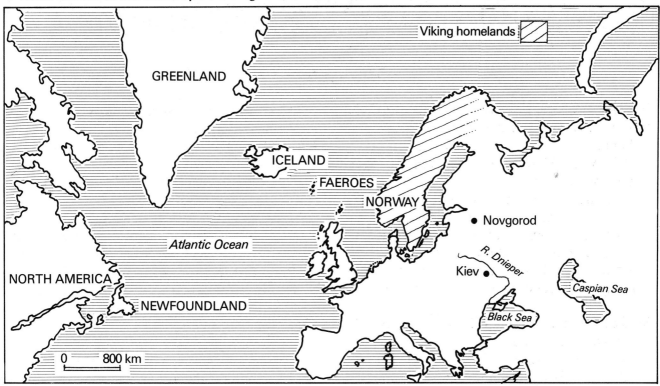
▼ Lands discovered and settled by the Vikings in the North Atlantic

Charles the Bald. They demanded 2,250 kg of silver for their trouble. Charles the Bald died, and his successor, Charles the Simple, decided it would be cheaper to hand over the northern part of his kingdom to the Danes altogether. So in 911 he made the Danish commander, Rollo, a duke, and gave him the whole of Normandy to rule.

# The Danes in England

The Danish Vikings also attacked England. At first they came on raids. Their boats sped across the North Sea, and drove in towards a smoothly shelving beach. As soon as the keel of the boat touched the shore, the warriors jumped out into the shallow water and waded up the beach. A few stayed behind to guard the boats, but the rest went inland looking for a village or a monastery to loot. They attacked Lindisfarne in 793 and Wearmouth and Jarrow a year later.

Like Egil, they stole, burnt and killed. Sometimes they also took prisoners to serve as slaves in Denmark. Then they raced back to their ships carrying their booty with them, and sailed away.

The Anglo-Saxon villagers were helpless. The population of a single village was too small to fight against two boatloads of Viking warriors.

The villagers sent messages to neighbouring villages asking for help, but it took a long time for the messengers to get through and for the men to arm themselves and march to the place where the Danes had landed. By the time help arrived, the Danes had ransacked the village and gone. In despair, Anglo-Saxon villagers on the east coast prayed, 'From the fury of the Northmen, good Lord, deliver us.'

**The Danes begin to stay**
Sometimes the raiding Danes went straight back to Denmark. But occasionally they found a small island in shallow water at the mouth of a river where their own ships could sail, but others would run aground. They would often camp on such islands for several days, sending out parties to raid nearby villages. When they

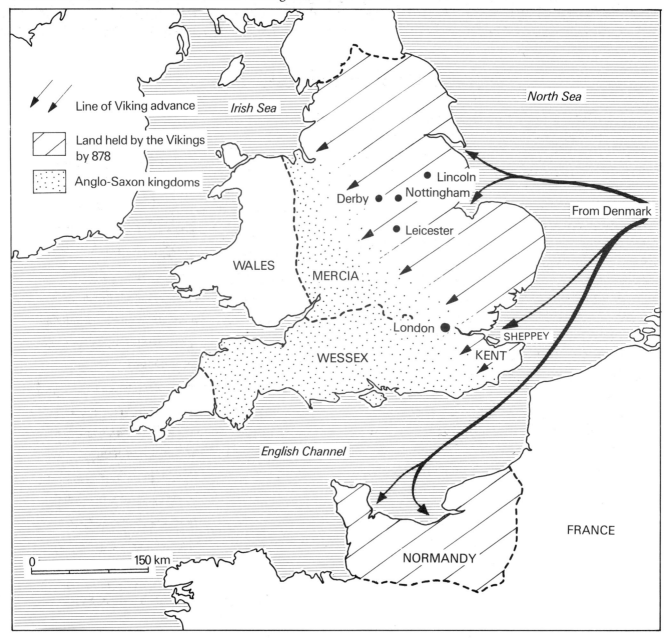

▼ Southern Britain and northern France in Viking times

**Legend:**
- Line of Viking advance
- Land held by the Vikings by 878
- Anglo-Saxon kingdoms

Irish Sea · North Sea · From Denmark · Lincoln · Nottingham · Derby · Leicester · WALES · MERCIA · London · WESSEX · SHEPPEY · KENT · English Channel · NORMANDY · FRANCE

0 ——— 150 km

---

had enough booty, they set sail for home.

As the years went by the raids continued and the Danes spent more and more time on islands off the English coast. In 855, for the first time, a Danish band spent the whole winter on the Isle of Sheppey in the mouth of the Thames.

### A Danish army comes to England

In 865, the Danes decided to settle in England. A large army, commanded by Ivar the Boneless and his brother Halfdan, landed in East Anglia. The Danish army moved inland. They captured the towns of Lincoln, Leicester, Nottingham and Derby. Then they turned north, and defeated the Northumbrians. The Danish army now controlled the whole of the north and east of England.

As soon as the Danish army had defeated the Anglo-Saxons, whole families came across the North Sea with animals, tools and seed corn to settle in England. They did not try to take land from the Anglo-Saxons. Instead they cleared and cultivated new land, and set up villages of their own.

# Study

## Making a chronicle

When we are trying to remember something that happened in the past, we often say, 'That was the year when . . .' This reminds us of other things that happened in the same year. Think of one example.

When King Alfred (see page 75) ruled Wessex the monks wrote down the events by which they remembered each year. This is called 'keeping a chronicle'. Sometimes the memorable event was a royal marriage or a battle. Quite often it was a Danish raid or invasion. One entry says:

> 789—A small fleet of Danes, numbering three ships, came to the coast and this was their first coming.

The chronicler goes on to describe how these Danes killed an officer of the King of Wessex, who thought they were peaceful traders.

Not all travellers from overseas were unfriendly.

> 891—Three Irishmen landed on the coast of Cornwall. They were starving. It had taken them a week to drift across the sea in a boat made of skin. This was because they had left their oars behind on purpose. They wanted to serve God and believed that he would send the boat wherever he wanted it to go.

1 Write an entry for the chronicle for each of the following years:
   793   855   865
2 Write an entry describing how a Viking fleet landed on the coast, raided a monastery, killed the monks, stole the silver and burned the books.

▲ Anglo-Saxon was very different from modern English. This is a section of the Anglo-Saxon Chronicle

3 Write an entry describing how strangers from the sea arrived, speaking a language that no one understood and behaving in a suspicious way. Did their visit end peacefully or violently?

### The Danes settle in England

When they had settled down and begun to farm their land, the Danes lived at peace. Nevertheless, the Anglo-Saxons were frightened and suspicious. But as time passed they became used to having a Danish village in the neighbourhood.

Eventually people from the two communities met. At first it was only to buy and sell. The Danes and the Anglo-Saxons came from neighbouring countries—Denmark and Germany—and their languages were very similar. For example the Danes called a cow a 'ku' and seed 'saed'. The people found they could understand one another quite well, and soon

73

► In this area, to the east of Leicester, Viking villages—Barkby, Barkby Thorpe, Beeby and Scraptoft—were built close to Anglo-Saxon villages—Syston, Keyham, Queniborough and Hamilton. Keyham means 'Caega's village'

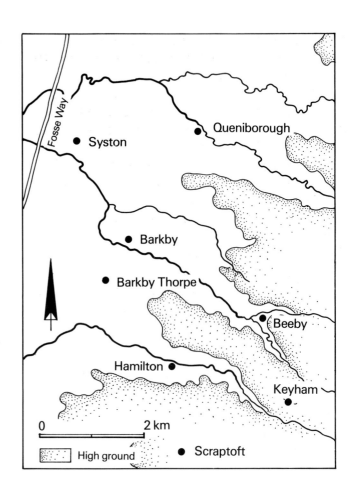

they were talking freely about crops and animals. The Danes explained how they farmed back in Denmark, and then listened while the Anglo-Saxons told them which crops and animals would do best in England.

Priests visited the Danish villages, and found that the Danes were quite willing to become Christians. They were baptised, built churches, and soon had priests of their own.

Some of the young Danish farmers married Anglo-Saxon brides who came to live with their husbands in the Danish villages, while a few Danish girls left home to marry Anglo-Saxons. So the two people mixed together.

Within a hundred years the descendants of the Danes were speaking Anglo-Saxon, and thought of themselves as English. Everywhere the Vikings settled the same kind of thing happened. The descendants of the Danes who went to live in Normandy in northern France spoke French. They knew no Danish at all.

# Study

## Saxons and Danes in the English Midlands

Draw the above map of settlements in the Midlands. Underline the Saxon and Danish settlements in different colours.

1 (a) Which village was founded by Caega, the Saxon?
(b) Which village was founded by Bark, the Dane?
(c) Which letters at the end of a place name tell you that it was once a Danish homestead?

2 (a) Why may Bark have decided to build his homestead by the river?
(b) Name the two other Danish settlements that were built near this river.
(c) Name the Dane who built his house about 3 km to the south of the river.

3 (a) The settlers at Beeby kept bees. What might they have traded with the Saxons and Danes who lived nearby?
(b) Which Saxon village would Scrap have walked through or near if he went to Barkby?
(c) If he walked at the rate of 3 km an hour, how long would his journey to Barkby have taken him?

Imagine what one of the following would have looked like and then draw it.
    Scrap's **toft**
    The homestead at Beeby
    Bark and his family building their first home in England for themselves and their animals

74

## King Alfred checks the Danish invaders

While Danish families were crossing the sea to settle in eastern England the Danish army was pushing west into the Kingdom of Wessex. As a rule the army fought only in summer when the days were long and food was plentiful. In the winter the Danes stayed in camp, protected from attack by a stout wooden stockade, while the Anglo-Saxons sent all their troops home to their villages until spring.

In the middle of winter 878, however, the Danes suddenly left their camp and marched deep into Wessex. There was nobody to stop them, and Alfred, the young King of Wessex, had to flee with a few men to hide in the marshes near Athelney, where he built a small wooden fort.

Here he was safe. His men knew the paths over the boggy ground. The Danes did not. They sent small patrols to explore and find the way. Alfred's men lay in wait for them, ambushed them and killed them. The Danes decided to build a camp and wait until summer before they attacked.

## Alfred defeats the Danes

This gave Alfred the time he needed. He sent messengers out from his stronghold to all the chiefs in Somerset, Wiltshire and Hampshire, telling them to bring their fighting men to meet him at Egbert's stone, east of Selwood, early in May.

The chiefs brought their men, and Alfred led them towards the Danish camp at Chippenham. The Danes came out to meet him, but Alfred defeated them at the battle of Edington, and forced them to retreat to their camp. He followed them and surrounded it. Soon the Danes began to run short of food. They begged for peace, and Alfred allowed some of their leaders to come out and negotiate.

Within a few days they had agreed on a treaty. Alfred allowed the Danes to leave their camp unharmed. In return their king, Guthrum, and the other chiefs promised to become Christians, and agreed to lead their army out of Wessex, never to return.

## Alfred's reforms

Guthrum kept his word, but Alfred knew that other Danish armies might attack his kingdom. So he decided to make Wessex stronger and easier to defend.

First he reorganised the army. In time of danger it was the custom to call all the able-bodied men from their farms and villages to defend the country. They could not stay away long, otherwise there was nobody to farm the land. So Alfred split his fighting men into two groups. Half stayed at home, while the other half went to fight. After a time the two groups changed places. In this way Alfred could keep an army in being for many months without the crops suffering.

Alfred also wanted to protect his people against sudden surprise attacks. So he set up a number of **burghs**. These were small towns surrounded by a wall and ditch which were easy to defend against the Danes. If a Danish army invaded, the people made their way to the nearest burgh and stayed behind its walls until the army went away again (see the picture on page 77).

Finally, Alfred decided to try to attack the Danes before they landed. He designed some large, fast ships to patrol the coast and drive away any Danish ships that came near.

◀ A silver penny (20 mm diameter) minted in King Alfred's reign. The inscription is 'Alfred re[x Sa]'. *Rex* is Latin for king

## Alfred and Guthrum divide England

When Alfred had made Wessex safe, he began to drive the Danes out of Mercia. In 886 he captured London. Once again Guthrum asked for a truce, and he and Alfred divided England into two. All the land north of Watling Street was given to the Danes (see the map below). It became known as the Danelaw. The rest, including London, belonged to Alfred.

This division did not last long. After Alfred died his son, Edward, conquered the Danes and took over the Danelaw. He was the first English king to rule the whole country as far as the borders with Wales and Scotland.

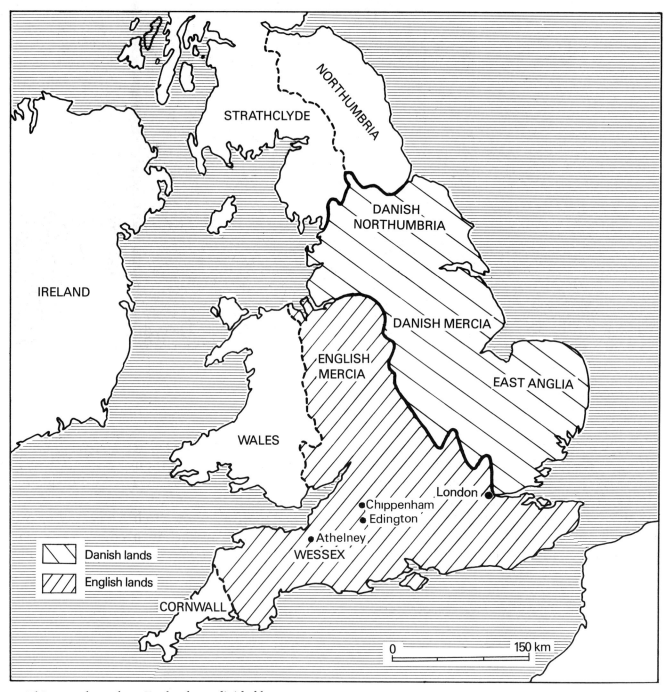

▲ This map shows how England was divided between Alfred and Guthrum, the Danish king, in 886

▲ Wallingford, in Berkshire, was one of Alfred's burghs. The line of his defences ran along the road on the left and, like the road, curved at each end towards the river, making a square

## Alfred in peacetime

Alfred was a great wartime leader. He could fight battles, organise armies and make treaties. He was also a great king in peacetime. He did his best to encourage learning. He founded schools, and learned Latin so that he could translate books into Anglo-Saxon for his people to read. He was also very religious, and set up several monasteries. Although he was often ill and in pain, Alfred was always good-tempered, fair and easy to approach.

'I wanted,' he wrote, 'to live worthily as long as I lived, and leave behind my memory in good works to the men who should come after me.'

# Study

## Writing a biography

**The work of Alfred**

A Viking poem says:

> Cattle die, kinsfolk die,
> One thing dies not,
> The name a good man leaves.

We still remember King Alfred, because a Welsh monk called Asser wrote his life story, or biography. His book tells us what kind of a man Alfred was, as well as what he did. Asser admired Alfred. If the King had any bad points, we are not told about them.

1 (a) Put these events in Alfred's life in chronological order, that is, the order in which they happened:

The capture of London
The Battle of Edington
The building of the fort at Athelney

(b) Give two examples of Alfred's work in peacetime.

2 Asser would have asked Alfred questions about his life.

(a) What answers might Alfred have given to these questions?

Why did you split the army in two?
What is a burgh?
How did you stop the Danes landing?

(b) To what question might Alfred have given this answer? 'I wanted to tell my people what the books said.'

3 (a) What do these points tell us about the kind of man Alfred was?

(i) He worked hard, even when ill.
(ii) He brought craftsmen from abroad to work in Wessex.

(b) Give an example to show how Alfred tried to be a good Christian.

(c) Do you think Alfred was a great king, even if he had some bad points? Give reasons for your answer.

**Danish kings in England**

Though Alfred and Edward defeated the Danes, it was not the end of the story. More Danish armies invaded England, and one of Alfred's descendants, Ethelred, tried to buy them off by paying them huge sums of money, known as Danegeld. But the Danes attacked again and again, and in 1013 Sven Forkbeard, King of Denmark, conquered the whole country and became king. He was the first man to rule over all the Anglo-Saxon kingdoms at once. He died in 1014, and his son, Canute, reigned from 1016 to 1035. So England became a Viking kingdom.

# Viking armies and Viking traders

## Viking armies

In the Viking kingdoms there were many forces like the Danish armies who conquered England. The kings and their chieftains all had bands of fighting men equipped with swords, shields and axes. Some were full-time soldiers. Others were sons of farmers who left the land for a few months to earn extra money. They were well trained, and the Viking warrior with his pointed helmet, thick leather tunic and battle-axe was feared and respected all over Europe.

The king's army was the largest, but if two or three of the most important men in the kingdom joined forces they could get a big enough army together to defeat him. In peacetime the armies

▲ A Viking warrior

were a nuisance. The men soon became bored and wandered round the country robbing and looting. But no king or chieftain dared to disband his army because he feared that if he did his enemies would attack him and take his land.

## Viking armies abroad

The Vikings were such famous soldiers that rulers of other countries would pay them well to fight on their side. As a result many Vikings went abroad to make their fortunes fighting for foreigners. Sometimes they went in ones and twos, but occasionally a whole army went together and hired themselves out to a foreign prince.

## Harald the Ruthless

The most famous army to do this was commanded by Harald the Ruthless, a relation of

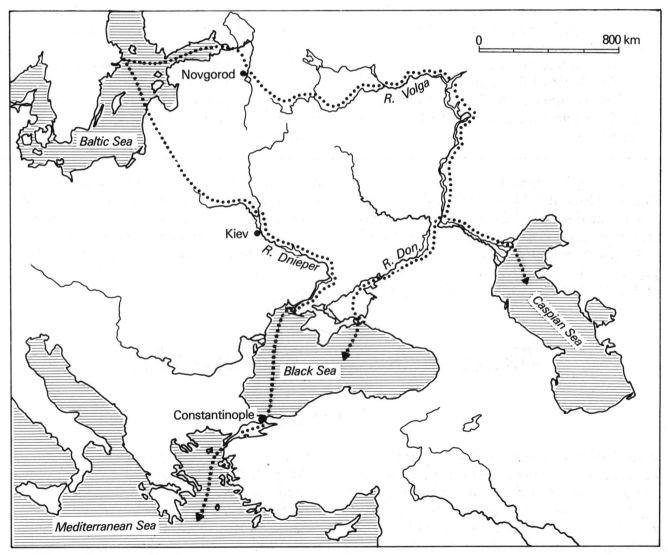

▲ Viking trade routes in Russia

79

the King of Norway. He and his men went all the way to Constantinople—now Istanbul—where they served the Emperor Michael for many years. They fought well, and the emperor paid them generously. In addition they robbed Michael's enemies. So they became very rich. Indeed, when Harald the Ruthless returned to Norway it was said that he had more gold with him than anyone there had ever seen before.

Harald eventually became King of Norway. In 1066 he invaded England, but his army was defeated and he was killed at the battle of Stamford Bridge in Yorkshire.

# Viking traders

### The Swedish traders

While the Vikings from Norway and Denmark were exploring by sea, the Swedes were trading in Russia. If the Vikings worked hard they could feed, clothe and house themselves. But they had no luxuries like gold, silver, silk or spices. They had to buy these from other countries. The trouble was that they had very little to sell in return. The Swedish traders got over this by stealing from other people.

### Russian trading posts

The Swedes invaded Russia and set up small fortified towns full of troops. Then they demanded regular payments of food, money, furs and slaves from the people of the area. As long as the people paid, the Vikings left them in peace. But if they refused the soldiers stormed out of the town and rampaged over the countryside stealing, kidnapping, killing and burning. The people found it easier to pay, and the Viking towns grew rich. Two of the most famous were Novgorod, in the north, and Kiev, in central Russia.

### The trip to Constantinople

Every year in May or early June the Viking merchants of Kiev, protected by a large number of armed guards, set out to sail down the river Dnieper to the Black Sea. Their boats were loaded with furs and slaves to sell in the markets of Constantinople.

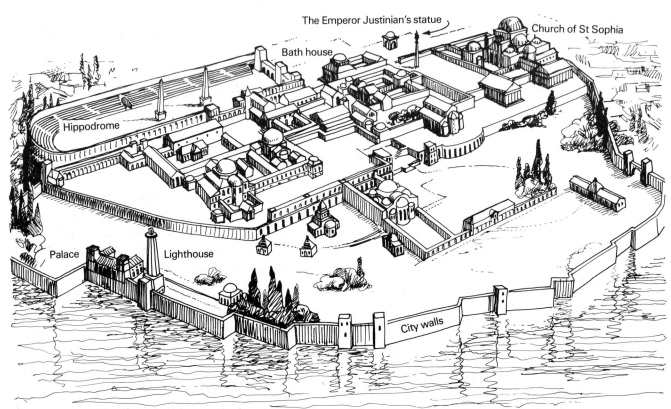

▲ Constantinople, with its towers and domes, was a great contrast to Viking towns

The voyage was difficult. The Dnieper had dangerous rapids. At one point the boats had to be unloaded and carried for several kilometres. But at last the little fleet reached the Black Sea, and sailed slowly along the coast to Constantinople, the capital of a rich and powerful empire.

### The city of Constantinople

The city of Constantinople was full of marvels. There were splendid churches and palaces, one of which, the Trichonchus Palace, was roofed with gold. In the emperor's palace there was a gilded metal tree with mechanical singing birds in its gleaming branches, while near the palace was the famous Hippodrome, where four-horse chariot races took place.

Many wealthy traders lived in Constantinople. They had gold, silver and silk in plenty and were prepared to exchange them for furs and slaves. So the Vikings sold everything they had, and, loaded with precious goods, made their way across the Black Sea and up the Dnieper to Kiev before the winter ice closed the river to their boats. In this way the Swedish merchants got the luxuries they wanted.

For two hundred years the Vikings fought, plundered, traded and explored from Newfoundland to the Caspian Sea. They changed the history of many countries, including Britain. But by the middle of the eleventh century they were settling down. At last they seemed to be content with what they had.

# Study

## Use your imagination

### Viking traders in the east

In about 912 an Arab, Ibn Fadlan, saw some Russian Vikings unloading their ship in Constantinople. He wrote: 'Each man carried bread, meat, onions, milk and beer and walked towards a tall wooden prop with a face on top .... The man casts himself down on the ground and says, "Oh Lord, I have come from afar with ... slaves and furs." Each man then puts the food at the foot of the idol, asking the god to send rich merchants to buy his goods.'

1 Vlad, a Viking captain, makes the voyage from Kiev to Constantinople. He and his men hope to make a large profit from selling their cargo. Write an account of their voyage.
*Things to write about:*
Vlad and his crew collect the slaves and furs
They sail down the Dnieper
They unload their cargo and pray to the god
(Think of some hard work that you have done to try to earn some money.)

2 Ibn Fadlan is in Constantinople on business. Write an account of how he watched a Viking crew unload their cargo and wait for customers.
*Things to write about:*
The Vikings unload their cargo and pray to the god
Ibn Fadlan's thoughts as he watches the rough, barbaric Vikings
Whether or not the Viking's prayers were answered
(Think of people you have seen behaving in what you thought was a strange way.)

3 Theodoric, a merchant of Constantinople, sells silk from China. Write an account of his meeting with Erik, a Russian Viking.
*Things to write about:*
Theodoric trades his silks for Erik's black fox furs
Theodoric shows Erik the wonders of Constantinople
Erik tells Theodoric about the Vikings' religious customs
(Think of a stranger whom you have enjoyed meeting.)

# Further work

## Discussion

1 In pairs, find three examples to prove each of the following statements:

The Vikings were plunderers.
The Vikings were traders.
Life in the Viking homelands was often hard.

2 Together, decide whether you agree or disagree with this statement:

> The Vikings had to become raiders and traders because their homelands were so poor.

Write down the reasons for your answer.

3 Begin your class discussion by getting someone to say 'I agree' or 'I disagree' and give the reasons why. Do the rest of you agree?

## Display

In groups of three, make a display on the topic 'Viking Explorers and Settlers'.

1 Look through pages 56 to 82 and choose a picture or map each.
2 Draw your picture or map and write a sentence under it, saying what it shows about:
(a) the reasons why the Vikings left their homes to explore or settle overseas;
(b) the seaways they explored and the countries they settled in;
(c) the date when they carried out their explorations and made their settlements.
For example, if you have drawn a Viking farmhouse you might write under it: 'After about 800 the Vikings needed more farmland so some of them settled overseas.'

## The Vikings in Britain

1 What do these Danish place names mean in English? (Use the glossary to help you.)
**by    toft    thorpe**
2 Why are many of the words used by the people of the Shetland Islands similar to Norwegian words?
3 Give examples of Danish words that were similar to Saxon words.
4 Draw a map to show how England was divided between the Danes and the Saxons by Alfred and Guthrum's treaty.

## Quiz: descriptions

1 A famous story tells how a Viking saved his life by solving riddles. Here are two of them:
> It flies high, has a whistling sound like the whirring of an eagle.
> Hard it is to touch.

*Answer:* an arrow.
> Who are those two who have ten feet, three eyes and one tail?

*Answer:* Odin, the one-eyed god and his eight-legged horse.
2 What does this describe?
> Built by the Romans, made of stone, used as a frontier.
3 Whom does this describe?
> Fought for an emperor, won a kingdom, died trying to become King of England.
4 Make up a 'Descriptions' question each. Choose someone to be in charge of the quiz. Give in your questions, divide into two teams and hold the quiz.

# 4  The Normans come to Britain

## William the Conqueror

### The death of King Edward

In January 1066 William, Duke of Normandy, heard some important news. Edward the Confessor, King of England, had died, and Harold, Earl of Wessex, had been crowned king in his place.

William was very angry. He was Edward's cousin, and Edward had promised him that he would be the next king. Harold had agreed, and only a year or so earlier had sworn a solemn oath that he would help William. So the duke felt he had good reason to be angry when he heard that Harold had seized the English throne.

### William plans to invade

William was a strong, determined man. He had been Duke of Normandy since he was eight and now, thirty years later, he was respected and feared by all who knew him.

He had set his heart on becoming King of England and he was not going to allow Harold to get the better of him. He decided to invade England, defeat Harold and seize the throne for himself. Many of his advisers thought this was a very dangerous plan. They pointed out that Harold was a good general and had a powerful army. William ignored them. He had made up his mind, and he set to work to organise the invasion.

### William prepares his forces

The preparations took a long time. William had to have ships, and soon tree-fellers and carpenters were busy cutting and shaping timber for the boats which were to carry the Normans

▲ A scene from the Bayeux Tapestry (see p. 87). Harold is promising to help William become King of England. The two chests that he is touching contain holy relics. William and his courtiers are watching

▲ The Norman ships, loaded with men and horses, cross the Channel to Pevensey. William's ship has a lantern fixed to the top of the mast to guide the others at night

▼ The Norman cavalry wore chain mail, which was made of small interlocking iron rings. The short bows carried by the archers could not shoot very far or very accurately

across the Channel.

William also had to find an army. This was not so difficult. England was a rich country. The land produced good crops, and King Harold and his nobles owned much gold and silver. Norman landowners knew that if they helped William to conquer England, he would reward them generously. So they promised to supply him with men to fight in his army, and to lend him money to hire others.

By August the men and the ships were ready. There were knights on horseback armed with swords and lances, infantry with swords and axes, and archers with bows and arrows. Many of the cavalry and infantry wore **chain mail** and carried long pointed shields. It was a good, well-equipped army, but for six weeks a strong north wind blew and prevented William setting sail for England.

**The Battle of Stamford Bridge**

Meanwhile in England King Harold was expecting William to invade, and kept an army in the south of England ready to repel him. But he had other problems as well. His brother, Tostig, rebelled against him, and made an alliance with Harald the Ruthless, King of Norway.

Harald also wanted to be King of England, and demanded that Harold should hand the country over to him. Harold replied that all he was prepared to give the King of Norway was 'seven feet of English earth for a grave, or perhaps a little more as he is a tall man'.

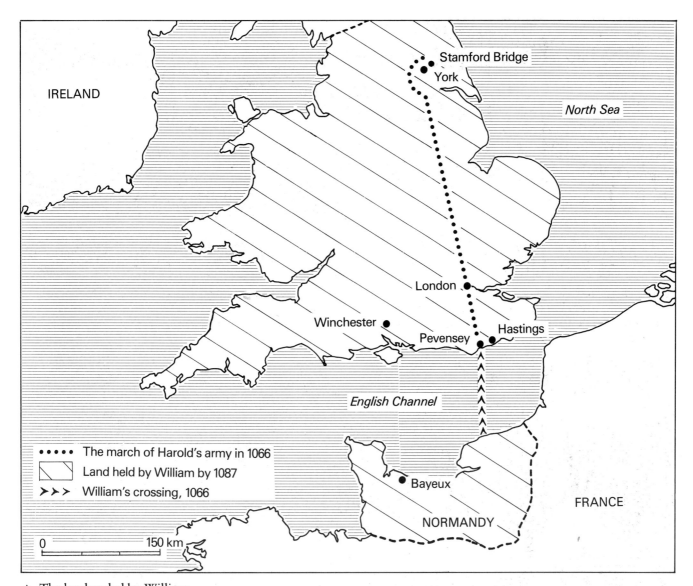

IRELAND

Stamford Bridge
York

North Sea

London

Winchester

Pevensey
Hastings

English Channel

•••• The march of Harold's army in 1066

Land held by William by 1087

➤➤➤ William's crossing, 1066

0        150 km

Bayeux

NORMANDY

FRANCE

▲ The lands ruled by William

In September 1066, Harald and Tostig invaded Yorkshire. Harold dashed north with his army and caught the Norwegians at Stamford Bridge on 25 September. There followed a desperate battle. Harold had the larger army, but the Norwegians fought on until all their leaders, including Harald and Tostig, had been killed. Then at last they fled to their ships and sailed back to Norway.

## William lands in England
On 27 September the wind in the English Channel changed. William loaded his army on to the boats and set sail. The next day they landed at Pevensey on the south coast of England. As William jumped from his ship he slipped and landed with his hands in the mud. A soldier standing nearby looked down at him and said,

'You've already got a grip on the soil of England, Duke, and will soon be king.'

Harold was still in Yorkshire, so there was nobody to oppose the Normans. William did not move far from where he had landed. He settled himself at Hastings, where he built a small castle. Every day he sent raiding parties out into the surrounding countryside, and they returned with hens, cattle, pigs and hay to keep the army and its horses supplied with food.

## Harold marches south
While William's army was resting at Hastings, Harold's men were marching south. Many of his best and bravest soldiers had been killed or wounded at Stamford Bridge, and the remainder were tired and needed a rest. But Harold would not wait. He could not rest until he had

swept William and his Norman army back into the sea.

So Harold and his men made their way down the Roman road from the north, calling on more soldiers to join them. By the time he reached Sussex on 14 October Harold probably had about 8,000 men, but many of them were poorly trained and badly equipped.

### The Battle of Hastings

When William heard that Harold's army was approaching, he got his own army together and set out to look for Harold.

He found him quite easily, on top of a small hill with a forest at his back. Harold's best fighting men stood in a line, their axes in one hand, and their shields held in front of them forming a kind of wall.

The Norman cavalry charged up the hill, but slowed down and were driven back before they could reach the top. Then the infantry tried. The same thing happened. Again and again the Normans attacked, but they were always forced to retreat.

At last after one attack some of Harold's army stormed down the hill to pursue the retreating Normans. It was a terrible mistake. As soon as they reached level ground the Norman cavalry rode at them and killed them.

There were now too few men left on top of the hill to drive off the Norman attacks. Slowly the exhausted English soldiers gave ground. Only a few men went on fighting. One of them was Harold. Eventually a Norman horseman struck him down and killed him. The battle was over.

### William is crowned king

Now that Harold was dead, there was nothing to stop William. With his army around him he made his way slowly to London where the English thanes accepted him as their king. On Christmas Day 1066 he was crowned in Westminster Abbey. It was less than a year since he had heard that Harold had seized the throne.

◀ The death of Harold. Historians used to think that Harold was the figure on the left, with the arrow in his eye. But now most historians agree that Harold is the man on the right, who has just been struck down by the swordsman on horseback

# Studying the story

## How do we know?

### The Bayeux Tapestry

Imagine a strip cartoon, 70 m long and half a metre deep, hanging on a grey stone wall. The pictures are bold and colourful. The writing that goes with them is large and clear.

Stand back and look at the seventy scenes that tell the story. First you can see Edward, King of England, seated on his throne. He seems to be sending Harold, a Saxon nobleman, with a message to William of Normandy.

Harold lands on the coast of Normandy and is taken to William. The two men appear to become friends. They go hunting together and when William goes to war with the Count of Britanny, Harold fights in the Norman army. Before Harold returns to England, he swears a most solemn oath that he will accept William as his lord and serve him faithfully.

Then the mood changes. Edward dies and is buried, but Harold does not send for William to become King of England as he had promised. Instead, he seizes the throne for himself. A great fleet of ships crosses the Channel, laden with knights and horses. Duke William lands in England to claim his rights.

On the day of the battle, the Norman knights ride full tilt against Harold and the Saxon army. Soon the ground is strewn with hacked and bleeding bodies. William is victorious and Harold, the traitor, lies dead, justly punished for breaking his oath. But many others have had to die also, because of his treachery.

If you now examined this great cartoon closely, you would find that eight strips of embroidered linen had been sewn together to form the tapestry. It was probably made in Canterbury and was first hung on the walls of Bayeux Cathedral, in Normandy, in 1087. Perhaps Odo, who was the Bishop of Bayeux

and William's half-brother, wanted to show that God had given victory to the Duke because the Norman cause was just. The Englishwomen of Canterbury put this Norman point of view into pictures with their needles and coloured threads.

1. (a) Is Bayeux in England or Normandy?
   (b) What was the name of the Bishop of Bayeux?
   (c) Why might you expect him to tell the story from William's point of view?
2. Study the scene from the Bayeux Tapestry on page 83.
   (a) What promise is Harold making to William?
   (b) What is he touching to show that the promise is sacred?
   (c) This scene is important. It justifies William's war against Harold from the Norman point of view. Explain why.
3. Study the scene from the Bayeux Tapestry on page 86.
   (a) Describe what you see in the picture.
   (b) Do all historians agree on what this scene shows?
   (c) Why might the meaning of the scene have been clearer to Normans who lived in 1087?

### The Anglo-Saxon Chronicle

One monk wrote in the Anglo-Saxon Chronicle that Edward changed his mind just before he died and left the throne to Harold.

1. Is it possible that Edward changed his mind? Give reasons for your answer.
2. From whom might the writer of the Chronicle have got his information?
3. Why may William have thought the throne should be his, even if Edward did change his mind?

$\rightarrow$

# Understanding what happened

Rewrite these events in the order in which they happened:

1 William and the Normans land at Pevensey.

2 Harold goes to Normandy. He promises to accept William as his lord.

3 Harold marches north and defeats Harald of Norway at the Battle of Stamford Bridge.

4 Edward dies and Harold is crowned King of England.

5 Harold marches south and is killed in a battle with William's army at Hastings.

### The time scale
1 Edward died in January 1066. How soon after his death was Harold's coronation?
2 Give two reasons why William did not invade England until September 1066.
3 What happened in Westminster Abbey on Christmas Day 1066?

### The battles
1 Why was there no Saxon army at Pevensey to stop the Normans landing?
2 Why were Harold's men tired by the time they reached Hastings?
3 What mistake did Harold's men make that gave victory to the Normans at Hastings?

# Further work

### Writing
1 Tell the story of Harold's visit to William in Normandy. Explain:

   Why Harold may have gone to Normandy to see William

   How they spent their time together

   The promise that Harold made to William and why it was sacred

2 Harold and his Saxons stand in line on top of the hill, ready for battle. Above their heads flies the dragon standard of Wessex and Harold's banner, 'The Fighting Man', embroidered in gold.

   Below, Duke William sits on his war-horse. His mounted knights wait for his order to attack. The battle is about to begin.

   Write an account of the Battle of Hastings as seen by either a Saxon thane *or* a Norman knight. Describe:

   The soldiers he saw lined up in the enemy army

   The main events of the battle

   What he thought and felt when he heard that Harold was dead

3 Write an essay in defence of Harold. Points to think about:

William may have refused to allow Harold to leave Normandy without taking the oath

What we are told in the Anglo-Saxon Chronicle

The Saxons were prepared to fight for Harold

### Drawing
1 Draw your version of one of the pictures in the Bayeux Tapestry. Write one or two sentences saying what your picture shows.
2 Draw a picture of something that happened in England in 1066 that is *not* shown on the Bayeux Tapestry. Write one or two sentences explaining why we need to know about this event if we want to understand what happened in that year.
3 Draw a strip cartoon of about six pictures, showing the events of 1066 from the English point of view. For example, you might include:

   Edward on his deathbed, leaving the throne to Harold

   The English nobles giving Harold their support

   The Battle of Stamford Bridge

**Group work**

1 Make a large strip cartoon to display on your classroom wall. As a class, choose seven or eight events in the story of William the Conqueror, from the time that he heard of Edward's death to his coronation on Christmas Day 1066. Write the list on the board.

2 (In groups of three or four)
Give each group a different event to illustrate, so that as much of the story is covered as possible.
Each group will need:
    a large sheet of paper
    several smaller sheets of plain paper
    coloured pencils
    glue

3 (In your groups)
(a) Study the pictures of the Bayeux Tapestry on page 84. Notice the borders at the top and bottom of the tapestry and the writing. Draw the borders on your large sheet of paper.
(b) On your smaller sheets of paper, draw bold, colourful pictures of people in your part of the story. Make it clear what they are doing, for example, chopping down trees to build a ship.
(c) Cut around your pictures. Give them to the most careful person in your group to stick on the large sheet of paper.
(d) Draw in the background of your picture, for example, the waves of the sea. In clear writing, explain what your picture shows.
(e) Display your pictures in the correct order to tell the story.

**Drama**
(a) Divide 'The Story of the Conquest' into about six parts.
(b) Divide the class into as many groups as there are parts to the story.
(c) Give each group a part of the story to prepare as a reading with sound effects.
(d) Choose one or two people in your group to be readers. The rest make the sound effects— for example: William's courtiers murmuring angrily; the sound of tree-felling; the horse's hoofbeats.
(e) Perform your reading or make a tape recording.

**What do you think?**
1 Did William have a good reason for invading England?
2 Was Harold a brave man?
3 Can we tell what happened in 1066 from studying the Bayeux Tapestry?
Give reasons for your answers.

# The Normans conquer England

The new King of England was tall and stout with a stern, unsmiling face, and a loud, hoarse voice. He was very religious, and attended several church services every day. He was obstinate, brave and a good organiser who made up his mind quickly and gave clear, simple orders which everybody could understand.

As Duke of Normandy, William had overcome rebellions and invasions, and by the time he invaded England in 1066 he was in complete control of his Duchy. But now he had to govern England as well.

**The revolt in the north**
When they heard that Harold was dead, most Englishmen accepted William as their king. But in 1069 a Danish army landed on the banks of the Humber, and many local people joined them to fight against the Normans. Together the Danes and the northerners attacked York and killed all the Normans they could find.

So in autumn 1069 William set out from London with his army and made his way north. He defeated the Danes and their allies, and everybody expected him to go back to London, for it was well into December. But William stayed in York for Christmas. Then in January he divided his army up into small bands and sent them out into the countryside with orders to kill every man, woman and child they could find, destroy all the cattle and sheep, smash all the tools, fire all the stocks of corn and burn down all the houses.

The soldiers did as they were told. From York they went north, killing, looting and burning until they reached the river Tyne. Most of the people fled from their villages when they heard that the army was coming and hid in the hills or the forests. This did them no good because when they got back home, cold and hungry, in the middle of winter, they found they had no houses, no animals, no food and no tools. So they starved. It was said at the time that 100,000 people died, and no crops were grown between York and Durham for nine years.

William was not usually so cruel. But he had two countries to rule and only a small army. A widespread rebellion while his back was turned might be very dangerous, and he decided in 1070 that if he punished the people of the north, it would strike such fear into the hearts of the rest of the English that they would never dare to rebel against him. He was right. At the end of his reign an English monk wrote, 'He was so stern and relentless a man that no one dared do anything against his will.' Even thieves were frightened, 'so that a rich man could travel safely throughout the country loaded down with gold,' wrote the monk.

## William's wealth and power

The conquest of England made William rich. On his way to London from Hastings he stopped at Winchester and went to the treasury where the kings of England kept their gold, silver and jewellery. William seized all this. In addition many English thanes tried to win his favour by giving him valuable presents, and monks handed over treasures from their monasteries. He also took money from every town he passed through. So he accumulated an enormous amount of money.

When William died in 1087 his treasure in Winchester was said to contain gold, about 30,000 kg of silver, and, according to a monk at Canterbury, 'costly robes, jewels and many other precious things'.

His conquest of England also made William very powerful. He could decide who should own the land, and could give all the important posts in the government and the Church to anyone he liked. As a rule he gave the land and the jobs to people who had served him well in Normandy and helped him to conquer England.

## The feudal system

When he granted land to someone, William expected something in return. The landowners, who were known as barons, had to promise to remain loyal to William, to pay him certain taxes, and to provide a fixed number of armed men to fight in William's army when needed.

A baron promised to be loyal to the king at an impressive ceremony known as doing homage. He knelt, unarmed and bareheaded, at the foot of the throne, and placed his hands between the king's hands. He then said: 'Hear, my lord; I become your man of life and limb and earthly worship. Faith and truth will I bear to you to live and die. So help me God.' Once he had done homage the baron could take over his land.

Most of the barons to whom William gave land already had estates. For instance, he granted much of Shropshire and land at Arundel in Sussex to Roger de Montgomery, who owned three large estates in Normandy. Roger could not look after all this land himself, so he granted some of it to his friends and servants. He gave some of his land in Shropshire to a knight called William Pantoul, a tenant of his in Normandy, who had fought with him at Hastings. In return for this land in Shropshire, William promised to pay Roger taxes and to come with his horse and armour to fight for Roger whenever he was needed.

William Pantoul, in his turn, granted land to the English peasants on his estate, on condition that they paid him some taxes, and spent some of their time working on his land.

This system of granting land in return for services and money was used all over Europe. It is known as the feudal system.

# Study

## People in the feudal system

1  Draw this diagram and fill in the gaps using the names of the people shown, the lands they held and the things they promised to pay or do.

*Promises he made*
To rule justly with the help of his barons

William the Conqueror
——————— of Normandy
King of ————————————

*Land he held after 1066*
Duchy of ——————————
————————————of England

To be loyal to William
To ———————————taxes to William
To bring armed men to ——————————— for William

Baron Roger de ———————

Estates in Normandy, and in ———————————and at Arundel in England

To pay ———————to Roger
To bring a ———————— and armour if Roger needed him

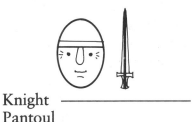

Knight ———————
Pantoul

Manors on Roger's estates in ———————————— and in England

To pay ———————————
To spend some time working on ————————— land

An English peasant

Land on William Pantoul's ——————————— in ———————————

2  Study your completed diagram, then answer these questions.

(a)  Who is the only man in the diagram who did *not* hold land in Normandy?

(b)  Why would the other three men have had to leave a servant in charge of their land sometimes?

(c)  Why did a feudal lord need to feel that he could trust the men under him?

## The castle-builders

At the beginning of William's reign there were very few Normans in England. They were afraid that the people of England might take advantage of this and try to drive them out of the country. So they built castles where they would be safe.

## Motte and bailey castles

The first castles were very simple—a tower on top of a mound, standing in a courtyard. The courtyard was surrounded by an earth bank with a wooden **palisade** on top of it. Outside the bank there was a ditch filled with water, or lined with sharp stakes. The Normans called the courtyard a **bailey**.

In one corner of the bailey, surrounded by a deep ditch, stood a mound of earth and stones. This was called a **motte**. Some mottes were as much as 40 m high, and 100 m wide at the top. Others were only about 15 m high and about the same across. But whatever the size of the motte,

its sides were smooth and steep—so steep that a horse could not possibly be ridden up it, and a man had to scramble up on all fours.

On top of the motte the Normans built a wooden tower two or three storeys high. This tower, which was often painted in bright colours such as red, green or blue, was called the **keep**.

Motte and bailey castles were a Norman invention. They were very useful. The bailey could be used for tethering horses or sheltering farm animals in case of attack. The keep had several uses. The ground floor was a store-room. Soldiers slept on the middle floor, while the baron and his family lived on the top floor. And as the roof of the keep rose high above the surrounding countryside, it was a splendid look-out post.

It did not take long to build a small motte and bailey castle. William the Conqueror built one at Pevensey and another at Hastings within a fortnight of his landing. The hardest work was

▲ The motte of Berkhamsted castle in Hertfordshire, photographed from inside the bailey. The fencing on top of the motte encloses the well shaft

building and consolidating the motte, and the Normans made local peasants do most of that. The wooden keeps were often constructed from ready-made timber sections.

## Castle sites

The Normans chose the sites of their castles very carefully. Sometimes, as at Windsor, they stood on a hill, but often they were on low, marshy ground, and relied on the swamp to protect them from attack. In the Middle Ages Kenilworth castle, near Warwick, was surrounded by about 40 ha of water.

Often the Normans wanted to build a castle in the middle of a town. At Oxford the townspeople had cottages on the best site. The Normans pulled the houses down, and built the motte on top of the ruins. At York in 1069 they accidentally set fire to most of the town when they tried to burn down houses which they thought stood too close to the walls of their new castle.

As the Normans settled down in England, they found they needed fewer castles, so they abandoned some of them. In time the keeps collapsed, the palisades rotted away, and grass grew over the mottes and ditches, but the remaining lumps and hollows often give a good idea of the shape and size of the original castle.

## Stone keeps

The Normans extended and strengthened the castles that remained. They pulled down the timber walls and replaced them with stone, and built towers to guard the gateway. They also built square stone keeps to replace the wooden ones. Some stone keeps were enormous. The Tower of London, built by King William, is 36 m long, 33 m wide and 27 m high. The walls are about 4 m thick. When it was finished it was painted white, so that it stood out clearly as the largest and strongest building in London.

Stone keeps usually had several floors. The lowest was used for storage. Sometimes the kitchen was on this floor too. Along one wall of the kitchen was a huge open fireplace, where joints of meat were roasted on spits in front of a roaring fire. A bread oven was built into one corner, and there was usually a pump connected to the castle well, which was under the keep.

Above the kitchen, and connected to it by a

▲ The Normans built the stone keep at Rochester in Kent between 1126 and 1137. From the tops of the towers at the four corners, the soldiers could see anyone trying to undermine the walls, and shot at them

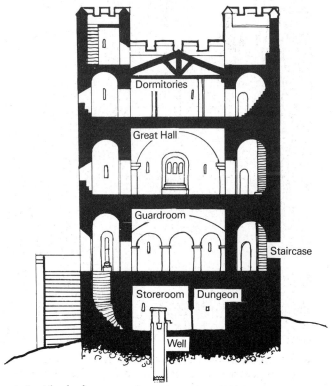

▲ Inside the keep

93

▲ A Norman baron

▲ A Norman noblewoman

spiral staircase, was the hall. This was the biggest room in the castle. It was furnished with tables and benches, and at one end there was a low platform where the baron and his guests sat to eat. The floor was strewn with rushes, and fireplaces with proper chimneys were built into the thickness of the walls. There was no glass in the windows, and when it was cold or windy wooden shutters were closed over them to keep out the draught.

On the next floor up there was often a chapel where a priest held regular services for the baron, his family and members of the garrison. The rooms of the baron and his family were usually on the top floor. Many of their rooms were small, so that they could be kept warm in winter, but some of them had window seats where the family could sit in the summer and admire the view. Even if the castle was attacked

▲ One of the main rooms in the keep of Hedingham castle in Essex, which was built in the middle of the twelfth century. Notice the round arches and the thickness of the wall beside the fireplace

▶ This plan of Corfe is based on one drawn in the sixteenth century. It shows how the whole village was dominated by the castle. Most of the houses were owned by masons who made their living working the local Purbeck marble

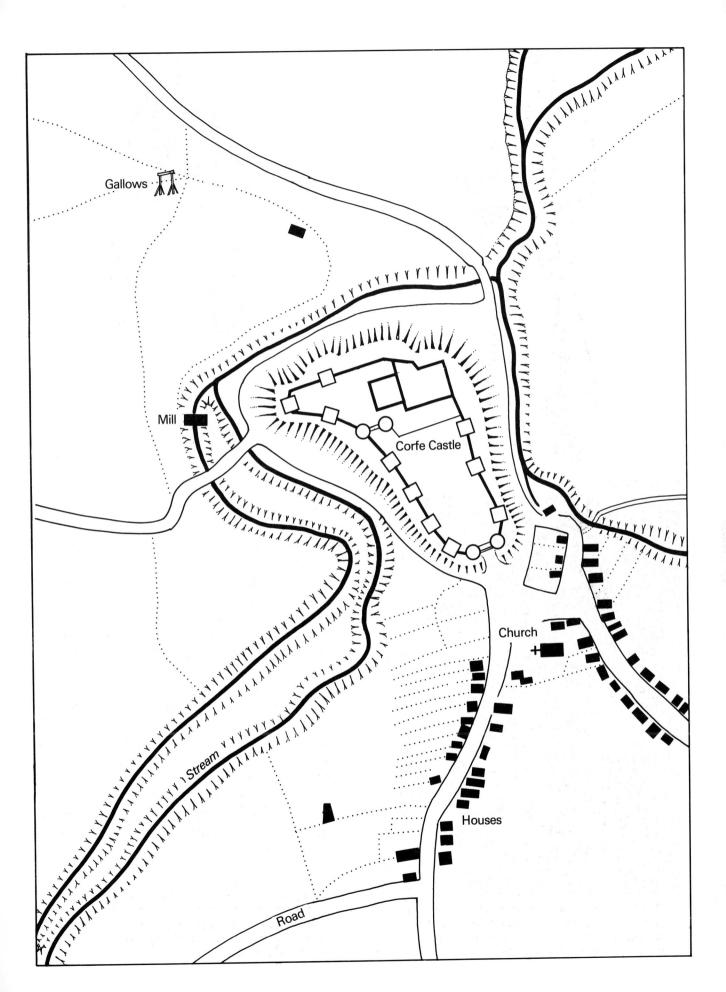

Gallows

Mill

Corfe Castle

Church

Houses

Stream

Road

95

they were safe, because the windows were so high that an arrow fired from the ground could not reach them.

When the baron was at home, the bare stone walls of his rooms were hung with curtains and tapestries, but when he was away the rooms looked cold and cheerless.

### The strength of a stone keep

Big stone keeps were too heavy to put on the top of earth mottes, so the Normans built them on level ground in the middle of the bailey. They were very easy to defend. In 1215 a hundred men-at-arms held the keep at Rochester in Kent for two months against King John and his whole army.

The only way into a keep was through a single small doorway, and inside there were narrow corridors and spiral staircases with room for only one person at a time to pass. Some keeps were divided into two by a thick stone wall down the middle, and at Rochester the garrison still held out in one half of the keep after King John had captured the other.

Once they had built their stone castles, the Normans knew they were safe. The English would never dare to attack them. Only a large, well-trained army with special equipment could capture a castle.

Many people liked the idea of living near a castle. If they were attacked they could go inside the castle for shelter, while the open area just outside the castle gate was a natural place for traders to set up a market or fair protected by the castle owner. Markets and fairs attracted more people to come and live in the neighbour-hood, and towns and villages grew up round some castles. Richmond in Yorkshire and Corfe in Dorset are two examples.

So a stone castle had many uses. It was a stronghold in case of attack. It was a barracks where soldiers could live, and the local baron used it as his home whenever he was in the area. In addition, the local court usually held its sittings there, and the men who ran the baron's estates used some of its rooms as offices. Finally, it was so strongly built that it made an ideal prison.

# William I and the Church in England

### Archbishop Lanfranc

As well as being able to hand out English land to his supporters, William could give them jobs in the Church. After 1066, as English churchmen died, he replaced them with Normans. For instance, in 1070, he made his friend, Lanfranc, Archbishop of Canterbury and appointed Thomas, one of his chaplains, Archbishop of York. Whenever an abbot in charge of an English monastery died, William always appointed a monk from a Norman abbey to take his place. Within a few years Normans held all the most important posts in the English Church.

Most of the men William chose to control the Church of England took their work seriously. Lanfranc was a very learned man who worked hard to make sure that all the clergy in England

▶ The south transept of Peterborough cathedral, built in the first half of the twelfth century. Norman churches had round arches and thick, plain columns

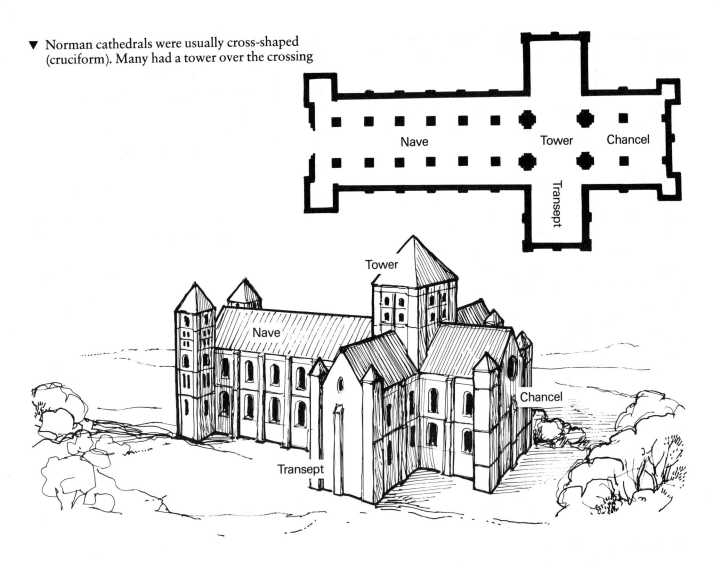

▼ Norman cathedrals were usually cross-shaped (cruciform). Many had a tower over the crossing

were obedient to the rules of the church and to the king. He sent copies of church regulations to all his bishops and ordered them to enforce the rules strictly. At Canterbury cathedral he drew up a new set of rules for the monks. The regulations were based on those of the abbey at Bec in Normandy, where Lanfranc had once been in charge. Many English monasteries copied the new rules.

## Church buildings

The Anglo-Saxons were not good builders. Most of their churches were small and many of them had been damaged or destroyed in the wars against the Danes.

The Normans were skilled builders. Their churches were bigger, and when they came to England they rebuilt many cathedrals, abbeys and parish churches in their own style.

Norman churches have thick walls and small windows with semi-circular tops. Inside there are huge round or square pillars, with semi-circular arches between them. The masons often decorated the stonework with patterns in red and white paint, and sometimes painted scenes illustrating stories from the Bible on parts of the walls.

Some of the abbeys and cathedrals built by the Normans were very large, and took many years to finish. Durham cathedral, begun in 1099, was not completed until 1133. Occasionally Norman builders made mistakes. The main tower of Winchester Cathedral fell down not long after it was finished because its foundations were on boggy ground. On the other hand many Norman churches and cathedrals still stand more than 800 years after they were first built. People still admire them because they are so strong and solid. At the end of the eleventh century they must have seemed very splendid indeed compared with the wooden buildings in which most people lived.

# Life under the Normans

## Norman England

After 1066 a Norman king governed the country, Norman barons owned the land, and Norman bishops ruled the Church. To help them do their work they brought assistants and secretaries from Normandy. With so many Normans coming to live in England, trade between England and Normandy increased. As a result, Norman merchants came over and settled in English towns in the south and midlands. Often they took over part of the English towns. They paid less tax than the English, and kept their own language and customs. The English townspeople often resented them. In 1086 the English inhabitants of Shrewsbury asked the king to reduce the amount of tax they had to pay. Part of the town was now occupied by forty-three French merchants who contributed nothing, which meant that everybody else had to pay more.

## The effects of the conquest

As a result of the conquest of England, Norman barons had more land, Norman churchmen had better jobs, and Norman merchants made more money by trading in England.

On the other hand, the only Englishmen who were better off after the conquest were slaves. They were all released because slavery was illegal under Norman law. Most Englishmen were much worse off than before. The thanes lost their land, and churchmen found that they were never promoted because all the best posts were reserved for Normans. Everywhere the Normans gave the orders. The English had to do as they were told and pay their taxes.

Their language suffered as well. Hardly anyone wrote in Anglo-Saxon any more. Churchmen used Latin and lawyers and civil servants wrote in French. So did poets and storytellers who wanted their works to be read at court, for the barons and their families all spoke French. They did not bother to learn Anglo-Saxon because they still had estates in Normandy, and spent many months at a time there.

For ordinary English villagers life did not change much. They still had to work on the land in the same way as before. Many of them did

▼ Sometimes the Normans made complicated carvings on doorways and other arches—dragons, serpents and climbing plants as well as human figures and geometric patterns

▲ These scenes from the margin of the Bayeux Tapestry show peasants ploughing, harrowing, sowing, and slinging stones at the birds

homage to their new lord and never set eyes on him again. They still took orders from the same reeve and went to the same church with the same priest in charge.

## The Domesday Book

It took William many years to put Normans in control all over England. One of his problems was that he did not know exactly how much land there was in the country, or how much it was worth. So at the end of 1085 he organised a survey. He sent men out to most parts of the country with orders to find out how much land there was, and who owned it. He also wanted to know how much it was worth, what taxes its owner paid, how many ploughs there were, and what animals the people kept.

In 1086 the commissioners set out. Wherever they went they called together ten or twelve local men, and made them swear to tell the truth. Then they asked their questions. They wrote down the answers and sent them to the nearest town. From there the information was sent to Winchester, where the king's clerks copied it into a book.

When the book was finished in 1087, William had more information about the country he ruled than any other king of his time. The book, which still exists, was called the Domesday Book because, according to one writer, it was like the Day of Judgement. Nobody escaped it,

▼ The Domesday entry for Birmingham, which was only a tiny village in the eleventh century. The clerks wrote in Latin, and shortened many words to save time and space. Here is a translation: 'From William FitzAnsculf Richard holds four hides in Birmingham. There is land for six ploughs. In the demesne is one, and five villeins and four bordars have two ploughs. Wood half a league long and two furlongs broad. It was and is worth twenty shillings'

*Hide:* about fifty hectares of land. *Demesne:* the baron's own farmland. *Villeins:* peasants who worked on the demesne in return for land. *Bordars:* peasants who worked on the demesne in return for a house

and it was fair to everybody. It was used for more than a hundred years to work out how much tax the owner of an estate ought to pay.

Scholars studying Domesday Book have worked out that in 1086 the king and his family held a fifth of the land, Norman barons had just under a half, and the Church just over a quarter. Only just over a twentieth was still owned by Saxon thanes.

# Study

## Making a survey

### The Domesday Book

The Domesday Book was a reference book for busy kings. Once all the information that William wanted had been collected and arranged in order, he and the Norman kings who followed him could easily look up a particular manor. Then they could work out how much the baron or knight who owned it should pay in taxes.

Today, historians look up the facts and figures in the Domesday Book to work out what life was like in Norman England.

No survey gives a completely true picture. The north of England, for example, was left out of the Domesday survey. The commissioners and scribes who collected and wrote up the information tried to be accurate and checked their work carefully, but they may have made some mistakes. Even so, the Domesday Book has been useful in one way or another for a thousand years.

1 Carry out the Domesday survey for Birmingham.

Copy the list of questions below in a list down your page.

Leave a space by each question for the answer.

> Who holds the land in Birmingham?
> Whom does he hold it from?
> How many hides are there?
> How many ploughs is there land for?
> How much woodland is there?

(a) Study the Domesday entry for Birmingham on page 99. Fill in the answers to the questions on your list.

(b) The king needed the answer to a particular question in order to work out how much tax the lord of the manor should pay.

  (i) Work out this question and add it to your list.

  (ii) Fill in the answer.

2 (a) What did the Norman kings work out from the information in the Domesday Book?

(b) Give an example to show how historians have used the information to find out about Norman England.

## The Normans in Wales and Scotland

For many years the kings of England had claimed to be 'overlords' of both Wales and Scotland, but in fact they had allowed the Welsh princes and the Scottish kings to rule their two countries as they pleased. William was not so easy-going.

### Wales

William controlled Wales by granting the land along the Welsh border to three of his most trusted barons. They were William FitzOsbern, whom he made Earl of Hereford; Roger de Montgomery, who became Earl of Shrewsbury; and Hugh d'Avranches, Earl of Chester. He allowed these three men to invade Wales and capture land for themselves. Gradually the amount of land in Wales owned by the Normans increased.

### Scotland

Scotland was a different matter. The King of Scots, Malcolm Canmore (meaning Bighead), was a rough fighting man who was always greedy for money and land. In 1068 he welcomed the nearest relatives of Edward the Confessor, Prince Edgar and his sister Margaret, to Scotland. Then, in 1070, Malcolm invaded Northumberland. The local earl, Gospatrick, drove him back. Shortly afterwards, King Malcolm married Princess Margaret.

▲ This carved figure on the doorway of Kilpeck church in Herefordshire is thought to be a Welsh warrior

This marriage annoyed King William. He thought that Malcolm might try to claim the throne of England on behalf of his wife and any children they might have. So he decided to teach Malcolm a lesson, and in 1072 he invaded Scotland. His army marched through the Lothians and crossed the river Forth. His fleet kept pace with him a few kilometres out to sea.

It was a very impressive force, and Malcolm knew he had no chance of beating it, so he met William at Abernethy on the Tay and made a treaty with him. He did homage to William, and promised not to invade England or shelter his enemies. He also handed over his own son, Duncan, to William as a hostage. William was satisfied, and took his army back to England.

For a few years, Malcolm kept his word, but in 1079 he again invaded Northumberland, burning crops and stealing cattle. This time William did not invade Scotland himself. Instead he sent his eldest son, Robert, with an army. Once again Malcolm did homage, and Robert retreated, leaving orders for a new castle to be built to guard a crossing point on the river Tyne.

In 1091, after William's death, Malcolm rampaged over the border for a third time. Once again a Norman army invaded Scotland and forced him to submit.

## The Normans and Scotland

In the meantime the Normans were increasing their power and influence in Scotland. Queen Margaret sent to Canterbury for Norman monks to come and work in Scotland, and all King Malcolm's sons spent several years at the Norman court. One of them, David, married a Norman noblewoman and became Earl of Huntingdon.

David and his brothers made many friends among the Normans at court. They took some of them back to Scotland, and gave them land. They used Norman fighting men in their armies, and appointed Normans to important posts in the Scottish government.

The kings of England hoped that all these Normans would use their power and influence to persuade the Scottish kings to stay on good terms with England. But there was to be fighting between the two countries for centuries.

▲ St Margaret's Chapel in Edinburgh castle. The chapel was built by Norman masons

# Study

## Putting the story together

### Using the Contents and Index

*The story of the Norman conquest of Britain*
Turn to page 83. Make a list of all the dates that you can find in the order that you come to them, until you reach this page again. As you can see, the events of the Norman conquest of Britain are not described in chronological order, that is, in the order in which they happened. Instead, the account moves around in time.

In real life, many events that form part of the same story may be happening at once, but when we tell a story we can only deal with one thing at a time. For example, when the Normans conquered Britain, some of their soldiers were fighting against the Scots and Welsh at the same time as others were building castles on the land that they had taken from the English.

The authors of this book could have described events chronologically, showing you how William defeated the English first and then went on to make himself overlord of much of Scotland and Wales. Instead, they first showed you how, over many years, the Normans made it impossible for the English to regain the lands they had lost. Then they went back in time and described how the Norman armies advanced to the north and west of Britain.

You can put the story of the Norman conquest into chronological order by using the *Contents page* at the beginning of this book and the *Index* at the end. With a little practice, you will see how you too can rearrange your information to tell the same story in a different way.

### Using the Contents and the Index together

*Turn to the Contents page* and find the section headed 'The Normans Conquer England'. Make a note of the page numbers at the beginning and end of this section. When you look up words in the *Index* for the work that follows, you will find the information you need between these pages. *Turn to the Index*, find the letter 'L' and the name 'London'. You will see that it is followed by several page numbers. Which pages will tell you about London at the time of the Normans?

Choose some more names in the *Index* and see what you can find out, from this book, about these people or places in Norman times. When you understand how the system works, go on to the questions below.

1  (a) Find the place names given below in the *Index* and note the page numbers that you need. Then look up each place on the pages given.

   Hastings   London   Abernethy

   (b) Write one or two sentences about each place saying (i) what happened in each of them; (ii) when it happened.

   (c) How many years passed between the Battle of Hastings and the Treaty of Abernethy?

2  The river Tyne flows through the border lands that the Scottish and English kings fought over.

   In the *Index* look up 'Tyne'. Read the pages given.

   (a) Why did William kill many of the people who lived between York and the Tyne?

   (b) What did his son Robert build on the banks of the Tyne?

   (c) Look up David of Scotland in the *Index*. Write one or two sentences, explaining why David was taken hostage, and how he later helped the Normans to increase their influence in Scotland.

3  Roger de Montgomery was one of William's most trusted barons. He helped to conquer England and part of Wales. In the *Index*, look up Roger de *Montgomery*. Read the pages given.

   (a) Where did Roger hold land before 1066?

   (b) Where did he hold land after 1066?

   (c) Why do you think that, long after Norman times, a county in Wales was named 'Montgomeryshire'?

▼ A charter drawn up in 1085 to grant land to Fécamp Abbey in Normandy. It was signed at the bottom with crosses by the king and by the important men who witnessed it. The biggest cross was made by William himself. The cross of his son, William, is on the left, the cross of Archbishop Lanfranc is in the middle. Most of the seal attached to the charter has disappeared

# A Norman king in England

Like the Anglo-Saxon kings, William I was always on the move, meeting his barons, checking that his officials were doing their jobs properly, settling disputes, and getting to know his kingdom. He ruled the whole of England and most of northern France. It was a huge area, divided in two by the English Channel.

William did not want to neglect either England or Normandy, so he spent about half his time in each. Between 1066 and 1087 he went back to Normandy seventeen times. Sometimes he was away for several years at a time, but usually it was only a matter of months. When he was in Normandy he left his half-brother, Bishop Odo of Bayeux, in charge of the government in England.

▲ The seal of William II shows the king on horseback. As soon as a king died his seal was broken, and a new one was made for his successor. The words round this one are: 'Willelmus Dei Gra Rex Angloru' (short for 'William, by the Grace of God King of the English')

## William's household

Wherever William went, he took a large number of people with him. He had a bodyguard of troops. Then there were his household servants. These included cooks and bakers; butlers and waiters; the constable who was in charge of his horses; the master of his wardrobe; and the tent-keepers. The marshal had to find lodgings for them all and the chamberlain, who looked after the king's money and jewels, had to pay all the bills.

The chancellor, who also went with him, was a very important official. He carried the king's seal, which had to be attached to every official document. William could not read or write, and neither could most of his barons. But they all knew what his seal looked like, and when they saw it fixed to a document, they knew it came from the king and was not a forgery. So the chancellor had to travel with the king, with a couple of clerks to write out any documents the king wanted.

All the officials had their own servants with them and, in addition, various barons and bishops went with the king to keep him company and give him advice. They also had their clerks and servants. So William moved about with a huge procession of men on horseback, and creaking carts loaded with baggage. His journeys were planned well in advance. He always had comfortable lodgings arranged in a castle, although many of his courtiers spent their nights in tents.

## William holds court

There were regular ceremonies on William's journeys. When he was in England he spent every Christmas at Gloucester, Easter at Winchester and Whitsun at Westminster. Then he

▲ Hunting was a popular sport with the nobles. Here Harold is shown riding with his hounds. He has a hawk on his wrist

sat in state, surrounded by his courtiers and wearing his rich robes and jewelled crown. At times like this new barons did homage to him, and new decrees were read out. They were splendid and impressive occasions.

Most of the time William worked hard, listening to complaints, giving orders, dictating letters and settling quarrels. If someone speaking Anglo-Saxon came before the king, he had to use an interpreter, for William spoke only French. He had tried to learn Anglo-Saxon, but had to give up. He said he did not have the time.

After only a few days in each place, the carts were packed and William was on the move again. Occasionally, news of a rebellion or an invasion meant that in the middle of a journey he suddenly had to ride off with a few of his most trusted barons to call out his army and fight a battle or besiege a castle.

## The Royal Forests

Sometimes William could relax. When he had time to spare he loved to go hunting, and he set aside huge areas of land where nobody was allowed to farm or kill any of the animals, so that when he wanted to hunt he could be sure of plenty of sport. These areas were known as Royal Forests, and anyone found poaching in them was severely punished. The king had

▲ William is sitting between his two half-brothers, Odo Bishop of Bayeux and Robert Mortain

many such forests. His favourite was at Wood-stock, near Oxford, and he had a hunting lodge built there for his hunting holidays.

## William's death

William continued his travels right up to his death. In 1087, sixty years old and enormously fat, he was on horseback in charge of his army at the siege of a French town. His horse suddenly stumbled, and William fell forward onto the iron pommel at the front of his saddle. He was terribly bruised, and the wound went septic. Six weeks later, on 9 September, he died.

His body was buried in St Stephen's church at Caen in Normandy. 'He was,' wrote an English chronicler, 'a very wise man, and very rich—more honourable and powerful than any of his predecessors. He was mild to good men who loved God, but incredibly severe to those who opposed him.'

## William's sons

William I left three sons. The eldest, Robert, was known as Curthose meaning short legs. The second, William, was called Rufus, or Red, because of the colour of his face; and the youngest, Henry, was nicknamed 'Beauclerk'—the good clerk—because he could read and write.

On his deathbed William I made a will, leaving Normandy to Robert, England to William, and £5,000 to Henry. This arrangement did not work. Robert went on a crusade, leaving William to govern Normandy as well as England. Then in 1100 William was shot and killed while hunting in the New Forest.

William's death may have been an accident, or it may have been a murder arranged by his brother Henry, who now became King Henry I of England. When Robert came back to Normandy after his crusade, Henry led an army against him, defeated him in battle, captured him and kept him prisoner for the rest of his life. So Henry, like his father, ruled both England and Normandy.

# Study

## Use your imagination

### The Normans in England

1 Fulla, a Saxon peasant, has been turned off his land. The forest where he once lived is now used by the king and his friends as a hunting ground. Anyone caught poaching the deer and wild boar that roam there may be blinded as a punishment. Write an account of the day when Fulla went poaching in the forest.

*Things to write about:*
Fulla kills a deer to feed his starving family
He hears the sound of a horn and hounds baying
He hides and sees the king ride by
*Either* How he is caught *or* how he escapes
What happens to him and his family
(Think of a time when you considered doing something for which you would have been punished if you had been caught.)

2 Rolf, a Norman wine merchant, is considering going to England and setting up business in Corfe. Write an account of how he tries to convince his wife, Jeanne, that she and their children will be safe from attack by the Saxons and that their business will prosper.

*Things to write about:*
Rolf describes the town of Corfe to Jeanne
He tells her about the Norman soldiers and masons she will meet there
The advantages that Rolf will have over English merchants
Jeanne's first reaction to the news and whether or not she agrees to go to Corfe
(Think of a country abroad and what the advantages and disadvantages of going to live there might be.)

3 King William is going to stay at Rochester castle for a few nights. His marshal goes ahead to make sure that there will be suitable lodgings for the King and his household. Write an account of how the marshal inspected the castle before the royal visit and the king's change of plan.

*Things to write about:*
The marshal's first sight of the keep
Rochester castle and the marshal's inspection
The king's arrival, followed by the baggage wagons
The news that made the king change his plans
(Think of preparations that you have had to make for an important visitor.)

# Further work

## Writing

1 An English chronicler wrote that William was 'severe to those who opposed him'. Make a list of three examples showing that William punished his enemies and his subjects severely when they opposed or disobeyed him.

2 What do the following points show about the kind of person that William was?

He invaded England because he thought he was the rightful king.

He ordered his officials to make the Domesday Book.

3 Choose one thing that William did and explain how it helped him to become powerful. For example, he made his barons pay homage to him before he granted them their land.

## Display—Norman skills

1 Divide into groups of three and in your group choose one of these statements:

Norman knights were trained horsemen.

Norman masons were skilled builders.

The Normans were good organisers.

(a) Find a picture in this book that illustrates the statement that you have chosen. Copy this picture, or part of it, on to a sheet of plain paper.

(b) Write one or two sentences under your drawing, explaining how this picture illustrates the statement. For example, under a drawing of the rounded arch in Hedingham keep, you might write, 'Only a skilled mason could cut the stone to build a rounded arch.'

(c) Display your work and compare it with the work of the rest of the class. Which group has shown the greatest skill in choosing and drawing its pictures?

## Proving your Point: the Normans in Britain

1 *England*

Find an example to support each of the following statements:

Norman landowners took most of the land away from the English thanes.

Norman priests and monks were given the best jobs in the English Church.

2 *Scotland*

(a) How did (i) Norman monks, (ii) Norman fighting men serve Margaret and David of Scotland?

(b) Did these monks and fighting men stop wars breaking out between the Scots and the English, as the kings of England hoped they would?

3 *Wales*

(a) Name the three earldoms that William set up on the borders of England and Wales.

(b) Why did William give these earldoms to men he could trust?

(c) The Normans conquered England rapidly. Why was their conquest of Wales slower?

## Quizzes

1 *True or false?*

The Danes invaded England three years after the Battle of Hastings.

The Normans made their buildings less draughty by putting glass in the windows.

Make up your own 'True or false?' quiz on the Normans.

2 *First to find the page*

Give the number of the page where we are told that *William I* was enormously fat when he died.

Give the number of the page where we are told that the tower of *Winchester* cathedral fell down because it was built on boggy ground.

3 Make up your own 'First to find the page' quiz.

(a) Look through the section on the Normans and write down two questions each, with the answers in brackets, on separate sheets of paper. Choose someone to be in charge of the quiz and give him or her your questions.

(b) Divide into two teams.

(c) The person in charge will ask the whole class a question. The first person to use the *Index* and find the correct page number scores a point for his or her team.

# 5 Henry II: The First Plantagenet King

## The death of Thomas Becket

### The king's anger

It was Christmas 1170, and Henry II, King of England, Duke of Normandy, Duke of Aquitaine and Count of Anjou, was with his court at Bures in Normandy.

The king's courtiers were having a miserable time because Henry was in a very bad temper. He had been upset by news from England. He had heard that the Archbishop of Canterbury, Thomas Becket, had defied him. The archbishop had refused Henry's request that Thomas should pardon three bishops who had taken part in a ceremony without his permission.

### Henry's quarrels with Becket

As a rule Henry would not have lost his temper over so small a matter, but it was not the first time Thomas had defied him. Thomas had once said that the king had no right to try clergymen in the ordinary courts of the land. He said that instead they should be tried by church courts where the penalties were much less severe. This quarrel had lasted for years, and Thomas had been forced to flee from England and take refuge with the King of France.

He had only just returned to England after a meeting with King Henry in France. The two men had agreed to forget their quarrel and work together as if nothing had happened. Yet as soon as Thomas set foot on English soil, he defied the king. It seemed that he was determined to cause trouble.

### Henry betrayed

To make matters worse, Henry had brought it all on himself. He had originally appointed Thomas as archbishop against the wishes of most of his advisers, and he had done it because he had believed that Thomas was his friend and would do as he wished. Instead Thomas had betrayed him.

As Henry thought what a fool he had been he felt his temper rising and he looked angrily round at his courtiers. They were frightened and uneasy, and tried to avoid his eye. This made the king even angrier, and at last he could contain himself no longer. 'What a set of idle cowards I keep in my kingdom,' he shouted, 'who allow me to be mocked so shamefully by a low-born priest!'

### The four barons set out for England

Most of his courtiers took no notice of what the king said, but that same night four of his barons, Hugh de Moreville, William de Tracy, Reginald Fitzurse and Richard le Breton, left Bures and secretly made their way to England.

As soon as they landed they made their way to Canterbury and went to the archbishop's lodging. Here they found Thomas at work with his advisers.

### Thomas defies the barons

The archbishop listened as the four angry men demanded that he pardon the bishops. He refused. Then they told him that Henry wanted him to leave the country. 'I did not return to flee again,' said Thomas.

Furious, the four barons left the room and went out into the courtyard to collect their swords and axes which they had left outside. When they returned they found the door barred against them, so they went round to the back of the building and battered with their axes at a shuttered window.

### Thomas goes to the cathedral

It was time for vespers. The archbishop, ignoring the din of the axes beating on the shutters and the shouts of his servants, made his way into the cathedral. Once he was inside some of the monks shut and barred the door. Thomas ordered them to open it. 'The church of God is not to be made into a fortress,' he said.

### The four barons burst in
A few minutes later the four armed men burst in, accompanied by other knights, all in armour and with swords and axes in their hands. It was now late in the winter afternoon, and the huge cathedral was dark except for the light cast by a few candles. The men-at-arms peered round but could see no sign of Becket. At last one of them shouted: 'Where is Thomas Becket, traitor to the king and the kingdom?' Thomas stepped forward out of the shadows. 'Here am I,' he answered, 'No traitor, but a priest and an archbishop.'

The four barons approached him. Once again they asked him to pardon the bishops. Again he refused. 'I have told you I will not change my mind,' he said.

▲ A picture of Becket's murder painted a short time after his death. The four barons are in armour and carry shields. One of them strikes Becket with his sword. Edward, the cross-bearer, stands at the back

### The barons kill Thomas
At this the four men rushed at Thomas. Reginald Fitzurse seized him and tried to drag him outside. Thomas flung him off. 'You wretch, Reginald,' he shouted, 'Take your hands off me. You and your gang must be mad to come here.'

Reginald raised his sword and struck the archbishop who now stood with his head bowed. His cross-bearer, Edward Grim, raised his arm to ward off the blow, and was cut to the bone. Edward staggered back, and William de Tracy gave the archbishop two mighty blows on the head with his sword, knocking him to the ground. As Thomas sank to the floor Richard le Breton struck him so hard that he sliced the top of his skull clean off, and the blade of the sword snapped in two as it hit the stone pavement.

As Thomas lay dead a man-at-arms stepped forward and prodded his head with his sword, spattering the floor with blood and brains. 'This traitor will not rise again,' he said, and they all turned and left the cathedral. They went next door to Thomas's house which they ransacked in search of gold, silver and fine fabrics. Then they rode away.

### The king is blamed for Thomas's murder
The brutal murder of Becket horrified everyone. Most people blamed Henry, and he admitted that it was his fault. He had wanted Becket out of the way, and when the four barons killed Thomas they believed they were obeying the king's orders.

In 1173, Thomas was made a saint. In 1174, in order to make his peace with the Pope, Henry walked barefoot through the streets of Canterbury. He knelt at the archbishop's tomb and was whipped by the monks as he prayed for God's pardon for his part in Thomas's death.

### The Canterbury pilgrims
Pilgrims went to Canterbury to pray to St Thomas. Some found that their prayers were answered. A few sick people who visited the shrine suddenly got better. News of these cures spread quickly, and for many years a steady stream of pilgrims went to Canterbury to pray to St Thomas for help.

# Studying the story

## How do we know?

### The evidence of the eye-witnesses

There is no doubt about who killed Thomas Becket. Several people saw what happened, including two monks, Edward Grim and William FitzStephen. When the knights burst into the cathedral, these monks were standing near the archbishop, helping him to conduct the service. Edward Grim was wounded in the fight that followed and William FitzStephen saw the archbishop die. From the evidence of these witnesses, we can reconstruct the events of that mid-winter afternoon in 1170.

### The picture in the manuscript

People throughout England were shocked when they heard about Becket's death. They wanted to know who had murdered him and exactly what had happened. Monks wrote to one another, exchanging information and comparing their opinions. Some of these letters were bound together in a book and an artist, whose name we do not know, drew a picture showing the murder. He would have based his impression of the scene on the accounts given by the eye-witnesses.

1 Study the picture of the murder on page 109.
   (a) How many knights are shown?
   (b) Are the same number of knights mentioned in the story?
   (c) What other details in the picture agree with the account given in the story?
   In your opinion, should we expect the story and the picture to agree? Give reasons for your answer.

2 (a) What happened to Edward Grim that shows he was near Becket when the struggle with the knights began?
   (b) Why may he *not* have seen the last part of the struggle?
   (c) What did Reginald Fitzurse do that suggests that he did not want to kill Becket in the cathedral?

## Understanding what happened

1 (a) Give the names of the four knights who murdered Becket.
   (b) What did King Henry say that made the four knights go to Canterbury?
   (c) What did Henry have to do in order to make his peace with the Pope?

2 (a) What did Henry and Becket quarrel about in 1170?
   (b) What had they quarrelled about earlier?
   (c) Why did Henry feel that Becket betrayed him, after being made Archbishop?
   In your opinion, why did the king need an archbishop who agreed with him?

3 One eye-witness wrote, 'It was evening, the long winter night was approaching, and the crypt was near at hand, where there were many dark and winding passages. There was also another door nearby, through which he could have climbed by a spiral staircase to the arched chambers in the roof ... But none of these ways of escape would he take.'

   (a) Was it possible for Becket to escape from his murderers? Give reasons for your answer.
   (b) *Did* he try to escape?
   (c) What reason did he give in the story for not barring the cathedral door?

### What do you think?

1 Is there any evidence to support the view that Becket deliberately helped to cause his own death? Give reasons for your answer.

2 Can we be certain that the knights came to Canterbury *meaning* to kill Becket? Give reasons for your answer.

3 (a) Give an example of something that was said, showing that it was difficult to see in the cathedral.
   (b) Why would it have been dark in the cathedral at that time of the day and year?
   (c) Why did the lighting cast shadows?

4 Why should we expect the eye-witness accounts to differ on some points?

# Further work

## Writing

1 Give an account of the murder of Thomas Becket as it might have been seen by Edward Grim. Describe:

How the knights hammered on the door of Becket's lodging house

How Becket and the monks went to the cathedral

How the knights came looking for Becket

The struggle that followed

2 Write an eye-witness account of the murder of Becket as it might have been given by Reginald Fitzurse. Include:

Reginald's reason for going to Canterbury

His conversation with Becket before the archbishop went to the cathedral

What Reginald meant to happen when he followed Becket

What did happen

3 Describe the scenes at Henry's court, as seen by a courtier, before and after the murder of Becket. Include:

The time of year and the preparations for Christmas

The news that made the king lose his temper

How the knights left the court

How the news of Becket's death was reported to Henry

What Henry did when he heard the news

## Drawing

1 (a) Copy the picture of Becket's death on page 109.

(b) Write two or three sentences explaining (i) who the people are; (ii) why murdering Becket in the cathedral made the knights' crime even more terrible.

2 Draw a picture that might be used for a modern history book, giving *your* impression of the murder of Becket.

3 Draw a set of pictures telling the story of the four knights. Start at Henry's court at Bures, and end with the knights looting Becket's lodgings after the murder.

## Drama

1 *Divide into groups of six* and decide who, in each group, will take these parts: the four knights, Becket, Edward Grim.

2 Write a play of three scenes, set in:

Henry's court at Bures

Becket's lodgings

Canterbury cathedral

*To help you*

(a) The story tells you something that was said in each of the places where your scenes take place. Write these words down first.

(b) Write down something that each character might have said either *before* or after the speech in the story.

(c) Learn your words and prepare your scenes.

(d) Choose two groups to perform their scenes to the class.

## What do you think?

What does the story show us about

knights and their weapons?

the rights of clergymen, compared with other people?

the authority of the Pope over the King of England?

Give reasons for your answers.

# Henry of Anjou becomes King of England

In 1135 Henry I, the last of William the Conqueror's sons, died. Henry's only son, William, had died in a shipwreck in 1120. His daughter, Matilda, was married to the Count of Anjou, Geoffrey Plantagenet, and lived in Normandy. Matilda claimed to be the rightful Queen of England, but most people at the time did not think that a woman was fit to rule. So Matilda's cousin Stephen became king. He was the son of William the Conqueror's daughter, Adela.

Matilda would not give up her claim to the throne. She kept control of Normandy and she and her son, Henry, invaded England several times. Finally, in 1153, Stephen promised that Henry should succeed him as king in place of his own son. Henry did not have long to wait. In 1154 Stephen died and Henry was crowned King Henry II.

## Henry II

When Henry became king he was twenty-one years old. He was of average height, but very strongly built and muscular. He had a red freckled face and short red hair. His eyes were grey and his voice, like that of his great-grandfather William, was hoarse. He usually dressed in Lincoln green and scarlet, with jewelled clasps at his throat and shoulder, and a richly ornamented buckle on his belt. Yet though his clothes were rich they were always creased and untidy.

Henry was immensely strong and full of energy. He could hunt all day with his courtiers and then spend half the night at work with his advisers. He was always busy. He strode about with quick, hurried steps, never resting. In church he paid no attention to the service. Instead he whispered orders to his servants, or drew in the margins of his prayer book. Even when listening to the evidence in a lawsuit he would mend a piece of harness, or sew up a split in a glove.

He was clever and well educated. He could read many languages, though he spoke only French and Latin. Above all, he understood the law, and was so good a judge that other kings asked him to settle disputes between them.

As a rule Henry was cheerful and good-humoured. Everywhere he went people came to see him, and pressed close round to get a good view. Sometimes he was pushed and jostled by the crowd, but he never seemed upset.

Occasionally, however, he did lose his temper. He grew angry when Becket refused to do as he wished and once when he heard somebody praise William the Lion, King of Scotland, with whom he was at war, Henry lost control of himself completely. He tore his clothes, ripped the cover from his bed and began gnawing at the straw in the mattress. On other occasions he chewed the rushes on the floor in his rage.

At such times people remembered the story that one of Henry's ancestors on his father's side had married Melusine, a daughter of the Devil. 'From the Devil they came: to the Devil they will return,' said one monk.

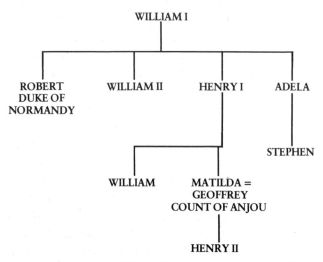

▲ A family tree of William the Conqueror's descendants

## Henry's territories

When Henry became King of England in 1154, he already ruled most of what is now France. In 1150 his mother Matilda gave him Normandy. In 1151 his father, Geoffrey, died and left Henry the counties of Maine, Touraine and Anjou. Then in 1152 Henry married Eleanor, Duchess of Aquitaine, who ruled a huge area in south-east France, which he took over. When he became King of England Henry's empire stretched from the Pyrenees to the Scottish border.

▼ Henry's empire stretched for more than 1,500 km
from north to south

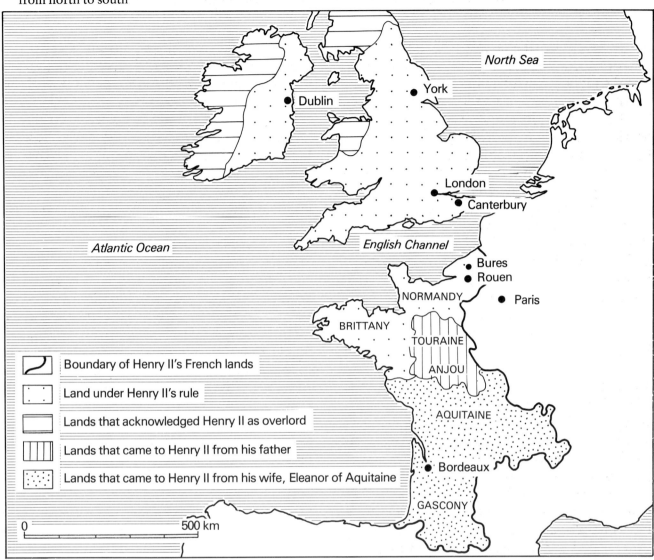

Life at Henry's court

Henry had a huge area to control. Like William the Conqueror he spent most of his life travelling. William had always planned his journeys very carefully, well in advance. Henry did not. He made up his mind on the spur of the moment.

This made life very difficult for the courtiers who had to travel with him. One of his secretaries wrote: 'If the king has said he will remain in a place all day, he is sure to upset all the arrangements by leaving early in the morning. Then you will see men dashing about as if they are mad beating their pack-horses and backing their carts into each other. It looks as if all Hell has broken loose.

'But if the king has ordered an early start he is bound to change his mind and sleep until midday. Then you will see the pack-horses loaded and waiting, the courtiers dozing and everybody grumbling. People go to ask the maids and footmen what the king means to do, for they are more likely to know than anyone else.'

Often a message would come from the king's quarters saying that he intended to spend the following night at a certain town. His courtiers would immediately send off servants on horseback to hire lodgings there. But half-way through the journey the king would suddenly turn off the route and stop somewhere completely different, where there was a comfortable house for him but nothing for anybody else.

▲ This side of Henry's seal shows the king on horseback.

▲ The other side of the seal shows him on his throne, with an orb and sceptre in his hands

'After wandering three or four miles through a strange forest,' wrote the secretary, 'we thought ourselves lucky if we found a filthy little hovel to stay in. To tell the truth I believe that he took a delight in seeing what a fix he put us in.'

The dignified barons and bishops who accompanied the king complained constantly. They said that to be with him was as bad as suffering the torments of Hell. But the king's unexpected journeys did have a good side. The fact that nobody quite knew when the king would pay them a visit or how long he would stay kept people on their toes.

# Henry II and the law

Henry's sudden changes of plan annoyed people who had legal disputes they wanted him to settle. Often they arrived with their case prepared only to find that the king had left the night before. Then they would have to follow him, and hope that one day they might be able to get him to sit and listen for long enough to make a decision. Some followed him about for weeks until their money ran out, and then had to go home with their case unheard. They knew that if they left all the details of a case with one of the king's clerks it might be years before Henry would look at them. Many people died with their cases still unheard.

When Henry became king there were many different kinds of law court in England. There were church courts which punished those who disobeyed the rules of the Church, and tried all clergymen, whatever they were accused of. The king had no power over these courts. They were controlled by the bishops and the Pope. In every county the sheriff, an official appointed by the king, held courts to punish those who broke the law in his county. And all the barons and knights had the right to hold courts to settle disputes among their tenants and punish those who had done wrong. The king himself heard only the most important cases.

### Henry's legal reforms

Henry did not like this situation. He believed that it was the king's job to administer the law and see that justice was done. It made him more powerful, and fines and fees brought in a lot of money. So Henry did his best to make sure that his courts heard more cases.

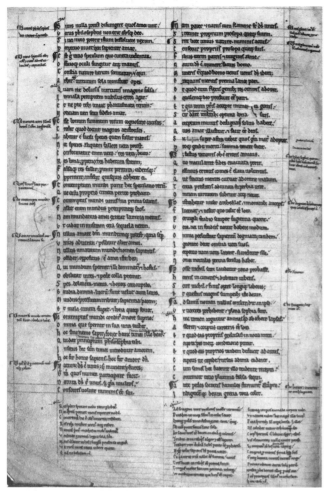

▲ There were many famous scholars in England in Henry's reign. This is a copy of a Latin poem by one of them, John of Salisbury, who became Bishop of Chartres, in France. It came from the Abbey library at St Albans

First he tried to take from the Church the right to try clergymen accused of offences like robbery and murder. This demand led to his quarrel with Becket, and the archbishop's death made most people side with the Church. So Henry gave up his attempt to try the clergy.

But Henry did make it easier for people to have their cases heard in the king's court. He divided the country into twelve regions and put a judge in charge of each with orders to travel round his district regularly and hear cases. This worked well, and was very popular. Fewer people now had to travel after the king. Instead they went to his judges. It was the beginning of the present system of Crown Courts.

## The Oxford heretics

Sometimes the king's courts and the church courts worked together. For instance, in 1166 Henry went to Oxford to pass judgement on some heretics. These were men and women who disagreed with the teaching of the Church. In the Middle Ages this was a serious crime. As a rule the church courts first tried to persuade heretics to change their minds and accept what the Church taught, but if they refused the judges declared them guilty of heresy and handed them over to the king's court to be punished.

The Oxford heretics of 1166 came from Germany. There were about thirty of them. Most were peasants and could not read or write. They did whatever their leader, a man named Gerard, told them. Gerard taught them that church services were useless. They did not believe in marriage or baptism. They refused to discuss their beliefs with anyone, and when they were threatened with punishment they laughed and quoted the Bible, saying, 'Blessed are they who are persecuted because they are righteous, for the Kingdom of Heaven is theirs.'

## The king's sentence on the heretics

The judges in the church court realised that nothing they could say would make the heretics change their minds, so they handed them over to the king. He sentenced the prisoners to be branded on the forehead, beaten and driven out of the city. He also forbade anyone to give them food or shelter.

The sentence was carried out, and as it was the middle of winter, all the heretics died of hunger and cold. Very few people at the time thought that this sentence was too severe. They believed it would prevent other people becoming heretics. If it did, it would have been well worthwhile, for the Church taught that all heretics would be damned, and would burn for ever in Hell-fire.

# Study

## Use your imagination

**Cases brought to the king's courts**

1 Stephen, a landowner, has quarrelled with his neighbour about the line of the boundary between their land. Write an account of how Stephen tried to put his case to the king.

*Things to write about:*

Stephen follows the king and his court

The reasons why Stephen never catches up with the king

Stephen's money runs out

The reforms that the king makes in the law courts

Whether or not Stephen wins his case

(Think of something that took a long time to put right because people in authority would not listen.)

2 King Henry is trying to persuade his archbishop, Thomas Becket, to reform the church courts. The king is angry because once Becket used to agree with him, but now he refuses to make any changes. Write an account of their quarrel.

*Things to write about:*

Henry argues that clergymen who have committed serious crimes should be tried by the king's courts

Becket puts his point of view about the church courts

Henry flies into a rage and sends the archbishop away

(Think of a quarrel you had with someone you thought was your friend.)

3 Gertrude and Herbert are living in Oxford when the German heretics come to settle there. They do not like what they see of the heretics' way of life or their views on Christianity. Write an account of the heretics' arrival, arrest and punishment as seen by Gertrude and Herbert.

*Things to write about:*

A heretic tells Gertrude and Herbert about his way of life and beliefs

The Germans are arrested, imprisoned and tried by King Henry

What Gertrude and Herbert think when they learn how the Germans have been punished

(Think how hard you find it to understand people whose way of life and beliefs seem to go against something that you believe in.)

▼ A London merchant

▼ A merchant's wife

# London—the capital of England

On his travels Henry often visited London, which he made the capital of England. Here he stayed at the Palace of Westminster, about three kilometres from the city itself. William I had built the palace to replace a much smaller Saxon building. His son William II built a huge hall. This still stands, though the rest of the palace has been rebuilt. Nearby stood Westminster Abbey, built in the Norman style by Edward the Confessor just before the conquest.

## The city of London

The road between Westminster and London was lined with houses, most of which had gardens planted with trees. To enter the city itself, you had to pass through a gate in the wall, which still followed the line of the old Roman fortification. At one end of the city stood the great white keep of the Tower of London. At the other there were two smaller strongholds— Baynard's castle and Montfichet castle.

The city itself was crowded and busy. There were thirteen monasteries and 126 parish churches. There were many large and impressive houses owned by barons or rich merchants. These houses stood on the main streets, which had sewers, and they had running water. There was also row upon row of small timber dwellings for tradespeople and their workers.

## Traders and shops

There were many trades in London. There were leather-workers, butchers, bakers, shoemakers, weavers, tailors, armourers, bridle-makers, goldsmiths and silversmiths. Down by the river the merchants had their warehouses.

Some of the traders were foreign. Frenchmen from Lorraine imported gold, jewels, wax and spices from the East, and wine and armour from the towns on the Rhine. Danes, Norwegians and Swedes sold timber, sailcloth and furs, while merchants from Rouen offered fish and wine.

Near the docks there was a famous shop where roasted or fried fish and meat were sold ready-cooked. The shop was open at all hours. It had cheap meat for the poor, and expensive dishes like venison or sturgeon for the rich. Tired, hungry travellers who had just arrived in London went there for refreshments, and housewives bought food there for unexpected visitors.

## Smithfield market

There were regular markets in London. The most exciting was the weekly animal market at Smithfield. Here, as well as pigs and cattle, horses of all kinds were on sale. There were cart-horses, pack-horses, placid, good-natured horses suitable for timid people to ride gently from place to place, and strong, fiery war-horses trained to carry a man-at-arms into battle.

The dealers went to a good deal of trouble to show off their horses. They washed them, brushed them and trotted them round to show how well they moved. They argued with one another as to which of them had the best mounts, and sometimes, on the spur of the moment, they organised races across the field to settle the argument.

▲ The great hall at Westminster, built by William II, now has new windows and a new roof, but it still has the original walls

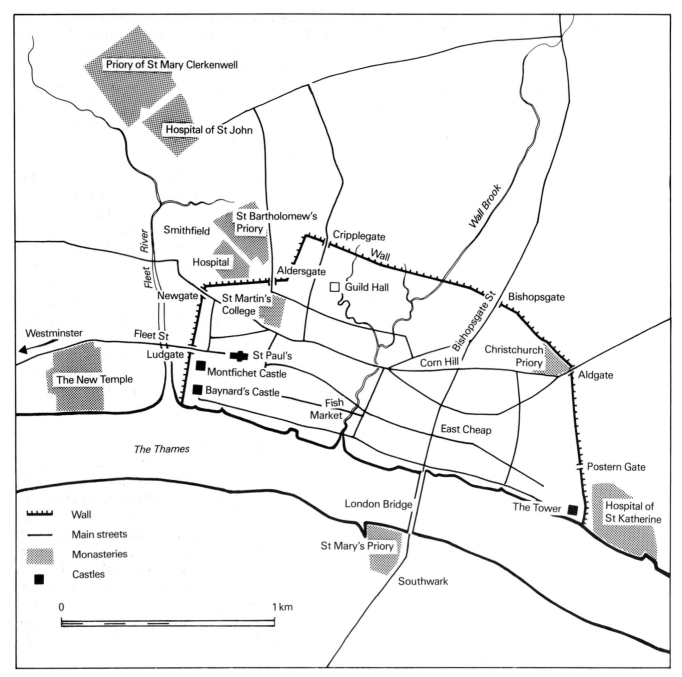

▲ London in the time of Henry II

## London schools

Many London churches had schools attached to them, where boys learned to read and write Latin. On saints' days there were debates and competitions between the various schools and every year, at carnival time, the boys took fighting cocks to school, and all the pupils spent the

▶ A London beggar. His feet were deformed and he had to use wooden supports

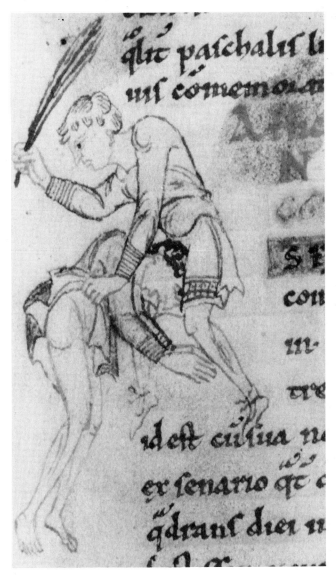

▲ An illustration from a medieval manuscript, showing a boy being punished by his teacher

shield was strapped to a pole sticking out of the water. Rowing boats charged down the river towards it. On each boat stood a boy with a lance. His aim was to hit the shield so hard in its centre that he broke his lance and at the same time stayed on his feet in the boat. In fact most of them ended up in the river, to the great delight of the spectators.

In the summer, on holidays, the city boys held all sorts of contests in the fields outside the town. They ran races, jumped, wrestled, put the shot and held archery competitions.

Londoners had to walk only a short distance to leave the town behind them. To the south, once they had crossed the old wooden bridge over the Thames and passed through Southwark, they were in open country. To the north there were rolling fields of crops and pasture, stretches of marshland and areas of forest. Londoners had the right to hunt and hawk in the countryside around the city, and in frosty weather they went sliding and skating on the frozen marshes.

### The fame of London

There were some drawbacks to living in London. A foreign visitor mentioned the enormous number of savage dogs roaming round St Paul's cathedral at night, and William Fitz-Stephen, who lived in London, complained about the danger from fire and 'the immoderate drinking of fools'. But in spite of this he still believed it was a fine place to live. He wrote that of all the cities in the world, London 'is the one that spreads its fame wider, sends its wealth and wares further, and lifts its head higher than all others'.

### Henry II and London

Certainly London was a rich and powerful city, and even kings treated it with respect. Henry I had allowed the Londoners to elect their own sheriff and justice. In other places the king appointed them. Henry II thought that the Londoners had too much power. He wanted to control the city. So he took away the rights granted by Henry I and appointed the sheriff and justice himself. The Londoners did not like it, but there was nothing they could do.

morning watching cock-fights. In the afternoon, teams from the schools went out into the fields and played very rough games of football. These were very popular. Crowds came out to watch, and elderly merchants on horseback remembered how they had played the same games when they were young.

### London sports

Every Sunday afternoon in Lent rich young men on horseback, carrying lances and shields, fought a mock battle outside the city gates. At Easter they made their way to the river, where a

# Study

## England's capital city

Of all the cities of the world, wrote William FitzStephen, 'London lifts its head higher than all the others'. He was exaggerating, but even so, London had become the chief or capital city of England.

There was always something to talk about in the capital. In the inns and lodging houses of the city, foreign and English merchants met to discuss business deals and strike bargains.

To the west of the streets and warehouses, on the banks of the Thames, the Norman kings rebuilt and enlarged the Palace of Westminster. Here, in the great hall, they held conferences with their barons on matters of government.

With so many visitors bringing news and new ideas to the city, the Londoners found plenty to argue about. They enjoyed a good discussion and met in the many churches of the city to hold debates, as well as services.

Boys who went to school in London (usually the sons of merchants and officials) were taught to keep to the point of an argument, and to win a debate by keeping their tempers.

### Holding a debate
*Choosing the motion*
The topics below might have been discussed in the reign of Henry II. Choose one of them as the subject or motion for your debate.
1 History tells us much more about the achievements of men than about women. This is because men are cleverer than women.
2 The Normans have done more good than harm since they conquered England.
3 It is a better life to be a London merchant than to be a feudal baron.

### Preparing your debate
1 Divide into two groups, one to argue for and one to argue against the motion. At this stage, do not make up your mind how you will finally vote. Wait until you have listened to the arguments and then decide whether or not the speakers have proved their points.
2 Make a list of three or more facts from this book which, in your opinion, prove your side of the argument.
3 Choose a chairman to be in charge of the debate and two speakers, one to speak in support of the motion, and one against it.

### Rules for the debate
1 The chairman says when the debate has begun and when it has ended. Anything said at any other time is not part of the debate.
2 When *both* main speakers have had their say, other people may join in the debate, but they may only speak if the chairman asks them to.
3 No one may raise a hand to speak while someone else is talking.
4 You may disagree with what someone has said, but you must say so politely.
5 At the end of the debate, a vote is taken and the chairman declares which side has won the debate. The losers clap the winners.

### Hints on winning a debate
1 Prepare your argument carefully and make sure that you can give facts to prove your point.
2 Listen carefully to what other people are saying. Are they *really* proving a point? If not, you must give the reasons *why* you think they are wrong.

# Henry II at war

Much of Henry's life was spent at war. For instance, he and the owners of neighbouring lands in France frequently quarrelled over where the boundary between their estates ran. Sometimes these arguments led to open warfare. If Henry invaded the country, his enemies usually took refuge in a castle. Sometimes it was so strong that Henry knew it would be very difficult for him to smash his way in. Then, as a rule, he would send a messenger under a flag of truce, offering to give up his claims to some of the disputed land. Often the rival baron accepted Henry's offer, the two sides made a treaty and Henry withdrew. But occasionally

▲ The main entrance to Chepstow castle was along a
▼ narrow passage between two towers. When the drawbridge was up, attackers had to get over a pit, through the drawbridge, through two portcullises and two thick wooden doors. The defenders fired arrows at them, dropped stones on them, and poured hot sand and boiling water over them. Distances on the figure are not to scale

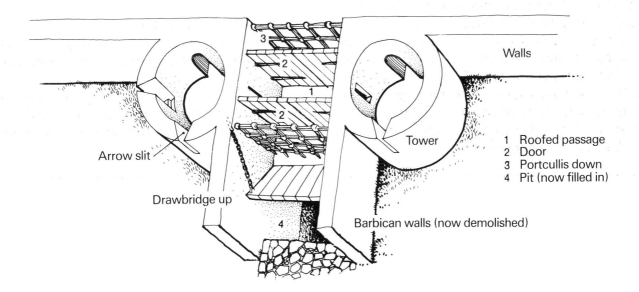

Walls

Arrow slit

Drawbridge up

Tower

Barbican walls (now demolished)

1 Roofed passage
2 Door
3 Portcullis down
4 Pit (now filled in)

▼ The round keep of Pembroke castle is very strong. The walls are 6 m thick at the base. The rectangular holes round the top are for the beams which held up an overhead platform

the baron refused and Henry had to try to capture the castle.

### Besieging a castle

Henry knew that there were several ways to take a castle. He could use his troops to surround it, and allow nobody to enter or leave until the people inside ran short of food or water and had to surrender or starve to death. But this took a long time because most castles had their own wells, and were well stocked with food. In 1266, when Kenilworth was besieged, it held out for nearly nine months.

Sometimes sickness cut a siege short. The supplies stored in the keep were often infested with rats and mice carrying dirt and disease. Occasionally the water was impure. In some castles the drains leaked into the well. If disease started, it spread quickly in the confined space of the keep. Men defending a castle feared sickness.

### Breaking down a castle's defences

Henry was always in a hurry, and could not afford to wait while the garrison of a castle starved or died of disease. So instead of besieging it, he always tried to find a weak point to attack. First, he looked at the main gate, but usually it was well defended with towers and drawbridges. So he examined the ground near the castle to see if it was suitable for tunnelling.

If the ground was firm, but not too rocky, he ordered some of his men to burrow under the walls, propping up the roof of their tunnel with pieces of timber. When they were right under the wall, they filled the tunnel with brushwood and set fire to it. The timber props burned through, and the roof of the tunnel fell in. Then flames burst from the ground, and part of the wall crashed down with a great roar, amid clouds of dust and smoke.

Mining, as this process was called, was sometimes very effective. In 1215, a mine brought

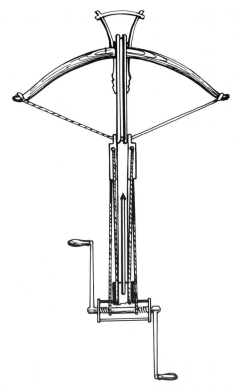

▲ Crossbows were made of metal. They were so strong that the string had to be wound back with a handle. They shot further than a wooden long bow, but they were slower to use

down a corner of the keep of Rochester castle in Kent, enabling King John to capture it. The easiest place to mine was at a corner, where Henry's men could drive wedges in behind the corner stones and lever them out. In this way they could gradually burrow their way through the wall. At first the defenders tried to prevent this by building wooden galleries which over-hung the walls. Standing on these galleries they could pour burning pitch, boiling oil and red-hot sand onto the men working below, or drop stones and shoot arrows at them. Eventually castle designers solved the problem by building round towers at every corner, so that there were no corner stones to remove.

Mining was impossible where the castle stood on solid rock, or was surrounded by wet and marshy ground. Where this was the case Henry had to attack the walls above ground level.

### Siege engines
Often Henry's men battered away at a short section of wall, hoping to knock it down. They had siege engines which could catapult huge

stones at the wall. These would weaken and eventually break it. They also had battering rams—tree trunks tipped with iron which were suspended from a wooden frame. Protected by a strong roof, up to a hundred men swung the ram backwards and forwards against the wall. But this took a long time because castle walls were made specially thick at the base to prevent the rams breaking through.

### Direct attacks
Sometimes Henry simply ordered his men to climb over the castle wall. This was the quickest way to capture a castle. It was also the most dangerous. While most of his men hurled stones from slings, shot arrows and fired crossbow bolts at the defenders on the top of the wall, a few ran forward with ladders, propped them

▲ A siege tower

123

▲ This young knight is receiving his sword from the king himself—a very rare honour

Once the attackers were on top of the castle walls, they could easily occupy the bailey. But they still had to capture the keep, whose walls were much too high to scale with ladders or towers. So they had to work away with their engines, picks and battering rams until they broke through the thick wall.

So it took a long time to capture a castle, and Henry rarely stayed until the end. He was too busy. As soon as his men were in position and the siege was under way he left, having been called away to solve a problem in some other part of his empire.

## Learning to fight

Henry took it for granted that he would spend much of his life at war. So did his barons. They knew that Henry might call them out at any time to fight at his side.

Barons and knights fought in armour on horseback. The horseman had to wield his sword or aim his lance and control the movement of his horse at the same time. This was very difficult, and took a long time to learn. So the sons of barons and knights began to learn how to fight when they were quite young. They played warlike games, rode horses, and fought each other with blunted swords and axes.

When they seemed skilful enough to fight in a real battle with their horse and armour, they were knighted.

## The ceremony of knighthood

The knighting of a young man was a solemn occasion. A skilled armed man on horseback could easily catch and kill unarmed men on foot. He therefore had the power of life and death over most people, and he had to promise to use this power unselfishly and to protect the weak and helpless.

So before he was knighted the young man spent a whole night in prayer. Then at dawn, to show that he was making a fresh start in life, he took a bath and put on a suit of new clothes. Next he was given his horse, armour, shield, spurs and lance. Lastly an old and respected knight solemnly handed him a sword. Once this was done the new knight was ready for battle.

Unfortunately many knights used their skill and strength for their own benefit, and not for the good of others.

against the wall and shinned up them as fast as they could.

Often the first ones to reach the top were struck down by a sword or an axe and fell to their death. Sometimes the defenders managed to push the whole ladder loaded with men away from the wall, sending it crashing to the ground. But occasionally enough men got onto the top of the wall to drive the defenders away.

If he had enough time Henry built a wooden tower the same height as the wall. He ordered his men to hang soaking wet animal skins on the tower to prevent it being set on fire. Then they filled the moat with bundles of wood, stationed armed men in the tower and pushed it on rollers up to the castle wall. When it was near enough the men stepped across onto the wall, driving the defenders before them.

# Henry in Wales, Scotland and Ireland

In 1157 Henry had to go to Wales. Owain Gwynedd, one of the Welsh princes, had taken over most of North Wales, including some of the land of the Earl of Chester. It even looked as if he might capture Chester itself. Henry decided to drive Owain out. So in June he wrote to his barons and told them to send him men and money to fight the Welsh.

He collected 2,000 knights, and enough money to hire a company of archers and buy supplies, including salt pork, grain, cheese and sixty casks of wine. He gathered his army together at Chester and drew up his plan of campaign.

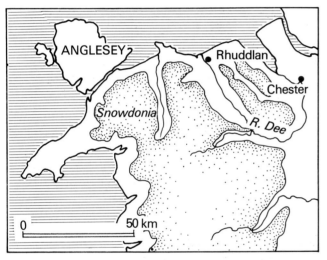

▲ North Wales and Chester in the reign of Henry II

## The march to Rhuddlan

Henry's first aim was to capture Rhuddlan, a castle built by the Earl of Chester but now in the hands of Owain. There were two routes he could take to get there. One way was flat and easy along the banks of the river Dee. The other lay over wooded hills.

Henry decided to split his army into two. He sent the knights on horseback along the river bank while he himself led the lightly armed men over the hills. Meanwhile he ordered his fleet to meet them all at Rhuddlan.

Henry's plan very nearly ended in disaster. The Welsh were waiting for him in the woods and suddenly attacked him and his army as they were marching along. There was a savage battle in which many of Henry's men were killed. This forced Henry to change his mind. He led his men out of the wood, and joined his knights who were riding along the river bank.

Owain knew that his lightly armed warriors would stand no chance if they tried to attack armoured knights and archers in the open, so as Henry advanced, the Welsh retreated.

At last Henry reached Rhuddlan where his fleet came to meet him. His captains told him that on their way they had stopped at the island of Anglesey to land a raiding party. The local people had banded together and driven them back to their ships.

## Henry makes a treaty

Henry and Owain now had a good deal of respect for each other. Owain had tried to frighten Henry off, but had failed, while Henry knew that Owain's men were fine warriors, difficult to defeat.

A truce was arranged, and in the end both men agreed on a peace treaty. Henry kept Rhuddlan, and built a new castle there. Owain promised not to invade the Earl of Chester's territory, and gave Henry hostages. In return Henry left Owain to do as he liked in the rest of North Wales.

Most of Henry's expeditions ended like this, with a treaty which gave a little to each side. Sometimes in later years the two sides argued about what the treaty meant and war broke out again, only to be ended by another treaty.

## William the Lion invades England

William the Lion, King of Scotland, claimed that he was the rightful owner of Northumberland. In 1173, while Henry was fighting in France, some of his barons in England rebelled against him. William thought this would be a good chance for him to capture Northumberland, so he led his army south and invaded England.

He did not dare attack Newcastle. The fortifications were too strong. Instead he besieged

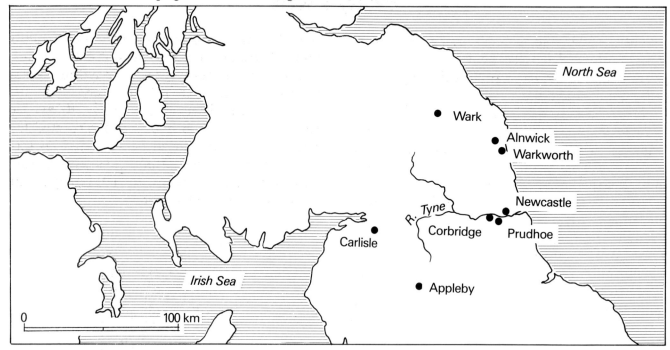

Carlisle, captured Appleby and attacked the castles at Wark, Warkworth and Prudhoe. The English gathered an army to fight him, and moved steadily north across the Tyne into Northumberland.

## William is captured

William was at Alnwick, besieging the castle. He had no idea that the English army was anywhere near, and sent most of his troops into the surrounding countryside to bring in supplies. He remained with a few knights outside the walls of Alnwick castle. Suddenly as he sat at dinner he heard shouts and war cries. It was the English army. After a short battle the Scots were defeated and William was captured.

By now Henry was back in England. On 27 July 1174, William the Lion, his feet chained together under the belly of his horse, was brought before him at Northampton. Henry imprisoned him in Falaise castle in Normandy. In December William accepted Henry as his overlord, did homage to him, gave him hostages and handed over five Scottish castles to the English. Henry then released him. There was no more trouble from Scotland as long as Henry was king.

## Henry and Ireland

In the twelfth century Ireland was divided into a number of kingdoms, each ruled by its own king. One of them, Dermot, King of Leinster, was driven out of his kingdom by the others. He went to Wales and asked Richard de Clare, nicknamed Strongbow, for his help.

Strongbow agreed to help on condition that Dermot allowed him to marry his daughter, and made him his heir. The two men got an army together and invaded Ireland. The Irish were no match for the Norman knights, and the invaders conquered almost the whole country. Then Dermot died, leaving Strongbow in charge.

Strongbow was so powerful that Henry feared he might try to set up an independent kingdom in Ireland. So in August 1171, Henry himself sailed over. All the Irish kings except Roderick of Connaught did homage to him, and Henry built several castles. In April 1172 he returned to England. He had shown that it was he and not Strongbow who was in charge in Ireland.

# Henry's sons

Henry and his queen, Eleanor, had five sons. One, William, died when he was a child, but the other four, Henry, Richard, Geoffrey and John, all grew to manhood.

Henry tried to use his elder sons to help him govern his huge empire, but they were never satisfied. They always wanted more land and more power. They quarrelled with one another and rebelled against their father. Eleanor encouraged them and Henry imprisoned her in Salisbury castle.

John, the youngest, was Henry's favourite son. In 1185, when John was nineteen, Henry made him Lord of Ireland. But when the prince went to Ireland he made fun of the Irish kings and pulled their beards, which were much longer than was the fashion in England and France. This annoyed them, and they banded together and drove John out of Ireland. John was very disappointed, and in 1189 he decided to join his brother Richard, who was at war with Henry.

## Henry's death

When Henry heard the news he was lying ill at Chinon in central France. War, travel and work had worn him out. He could not bear the thought that his youngest son had betrayed him. 'Now all the rest may go as it will,' he said, 'I care no more for myself or for anything else in the world.' On 6 July 1189 he died.

He had been King of England for thirty-five years, and had been feared and respected far and wide. But as soon as he was dead his servants tipped him out of bed, seized his jewels, his money and his clothes, and left him lying on the floor in his underwear.

▲ This statue of Henry II was carved shortly after his death and placed on his tomb

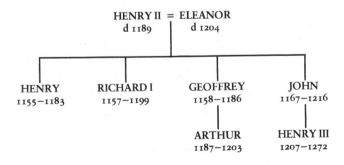

```
            HENRY II = ELEANOR
             d 1189    d 1204
    ┌───────────┬───────────┬───────────┐
  HENRY      RICHARD I    GEOFFREY      JOHN
 1155–1183   1157–1199    1158–1186   1167–1216
                             │            │
                          ARTHUR      HENRY III
                         1187–1203    1207–1272
```

▲ When Henry died in 1189 two of his sons, Henry and Geoffrey, were already dead. Only Richard and John were left alive

# Study

## Making a family tree

### Kingdoms—the king's property

In the middle ages a king thought of his kingdom as property that belonged to himself and his family. When he married he expected his wife to bring him more land and money to add to his wealth. When he died his land was divided between his sons and, sometimes, his daughters. Often, his children were dissatisfied with their inheritance, that is, the amount of land that their father left to each of them. They might even go to war with each other if they felt that they had been treated unfairly.

If a king had no children to follow him, several of his nephews or nieces might claim the throne. When this happened, all the claimants had to show how they were related to the rest of the family, and state why their claim was better than anyone else's. Those who could not prove their claim lost a kingdom. For this reason, the children of noble parents had to know who their ancestors were, and learned the names of their grandparents and great-grandparents by heart. They also had to know how they were related to other important families.

We need to know something about these noble families if we want to understand the times they lived in, but we can look at diagrams of their family trees, instead of learning them by heart. Many people today like to make their own family trees, usually because they want to find out more about the ancestors they are descended from, not because they hope to claim a throne.

1  Copy the sentences below and fill in the spaces by using these words correctly:

descendant ancestors wife inherited sons

Henry II _____ the kingdom of England and lands in France from his _____. When he married, his _____ brought him the Duchy of Aquitaine, and by the time he died, he had a large empire to leave to his sons and their _____.

2  (a)  How was Henry I related to (i) Stephen, (ii) Matilda?
(b)  What did Stephen and Matilda quarrel about when Henry I died?
(c)  Why did Matilda's son Henry inherit the throne instead of Stephen's son?

3  (a)  Copy the family tree of William the Conqueror on page 127.
(b)  Read the section on 'Henry's sons' on page 127.
It was said that Henry's father, Geoffrey, was descended from the Devil, and so his family was called 'The Devil's Brood'.
Draw the family tree of 'The Devil's Brood', beginning with Matilda and Geoffrey of Anjou and ending with the five sons of Henry and Eleanor of Aquitaine.
(c)  Give an example of something that Henry or one of his sons said or did that made people say that the family must be descended from the Devil.

# Further work

## Writing

1 Write out these sentences, filling in the spaces:

Knights had the power of life and death over most people because _____

A knight was not given his armour until he had spent a night in prayer and _____ _____ but some knights did not do their duty and used their power selfishly.

2 (a) Find two examples to prove each of the following points about King Henry:

> He had a violent temper.
>
> He was a tireless traveller.
>
> He believed that the king should see that justice was done.

(b) Use the examples you have found to write three paragraphs under the title, 'The character of King Henry II'.

(c) Write a final paragraph saying whether or not you think that Henry tried to be a good king. Give your reasons for thinking as you do.

3 (a) Make a list of four or five points to prove each of these statements:

> Life at the king's court was difficult for his courtiers.
>
> Life in a castle under attack was hard for the defenders.

(b) Write a paragraph of about half a page saying which you think was more dangerous, life at court, or life in a castle under attack. Give your reasons.

4 Answer the questions below in complete sentences.

Which part of Wales was Henry unable to seize from Owain Gwynedd?

Why did the Scots have to obey Henry after December 1174?

How did Henry stop Ireland becoming an independent kingdom?

Why, when Henry was King of England and overlord of most of Britain, did he spend so much time abroad?

## Drawing

1 (a) Read the description of Henry II on page 112 beginning 'When Henry became king'.

(b) Draw *your* idea of what the king looked like, based on this description.

2 (a) Read the description of life at Henry's court, page 113, beginning 'This made life very difficult for the courtiers'.

(b) Draw your idea of 'all Hell breaking loose', based on this description.

3 (a) Read the description of London schools on page 118, beginning 'Many of the London churches had schools'.

(b) Draw your idea of the spectators watching a rough football match.

Display your pictures and compare your ideas.

## Why did it matter?

1 Why did noble and royal families know so much about their family trees?

2 Why did the sons of knights and barons spend so much time practising fighting on horseback?

3 When might a rat seem as dangerous as a siege engine?

## Quiz: Who's who?

Name the people who are described below:

> He quarrelled with the King, fled to France, returned to England and was murdered in his own cathedral.

> The king's favourite son went to Ireland, made fun of the chiefs and rebelled against his father.

Make up your own 'Who's who?' quiz.

# —6 Inquiry: Roads to Camelot—

## Introduction: The Age of Invasions

The Roman army left Britain at the beginning of the fifth century. The next seven hundred years are often called 'The Age of Invasions'. Even before the Roman emperor recalled his legions to Italy, Anglo-Saxon warriors from Germany were raiding Britain. After the legions left the raiders became invaders. They seized much of the country and divided it into kingdoms. Their descendants learnt what it was like to be invaded when their lands were attacked by the Danes and Norwegians in the ninth century and by the Normans at the end of the eleventh century.

By AD 1100 the age of invasions was over. The various races of people who lived in the British Isles began to settle down together, though many of them still thought of themselves as Celts or Saxons, Danes or Normans. They knew that their ancestors had fought hard for the land that they now lived in and they did not forget old struggles easily. Each race remembered the heroes of the past who had battled for new territory or defended their people from attack, and their names were honoured in stories that grew and changed into legends.

## The legend of King Arthur

By the twelfth century, many legends had gathered around the name of one of these heroes, who was called King Arthur. This king, the legends said, was a brave leader who had protected his people when they were attacked by invaders. For many years, he kept peace throughout the whole country. Then his enemies rebelled against him. In the fierce battle that followed, Arthur's army was defeated and scattered. The last of his knights carried the dying king away from the field. Where Arthur was buried, no one knew.

All the people of Britain, whatever race they belonged to, respected the memory of this leader. According to the legends, he and his warriors fought honourably, respected women and protected the weak.

The legends do not tell us exactly when this king lived or where he fought his last great battle. We know that a British leader called Arthur lived in the fifth century and fought against the Saxon invaders. We know very little about this Arthur of history because the written records that deal with the time when he lived are difficult to interpret and may not be accurate. But whoever the real Arthur may have been, the King Arthur of legend became for many people a symbol of a brave king who ruled over a united kingdom.

## Camelot: an ideal city

As life became more settled and homes more comfortable, rich nobles hung tapestries on their walls, showing scenes from the stories of King Arthur. In these scenes the king and his courtiers walk through the palaces and gardens of a beautiful walled city. Knights ride out over the drawbridge to look for adventure. From the battlements above, their ladies throw flowers to them and wave goodbye. The people who looked at these tapestries saw the city that they would have liked to live in.

When the stories about Arthur were written down, the writers called this city 'Camelot'. We do not know why they chose this name. One of them may simply have made it up. But wherever the name came from, the idea of the city and its king became powerful in people's minds and influenced the way in which some of them behaved. There were many wars in the twelfth and thirteenth centuries, but honourable knights, like the knights in the stories, tried to limit the bloodshed and to spare innocent people. Famines and plagues caused hardship and suffering but men and women did not give up trying to make their cities beautiful to look at and safe to live in.

Was there ever a real Camelot? In each century since the stories were written down, some people have believed that there was once a city ruled by Arthur and have tried to find it. Some now think that its remains have been discovered. Others say that the stories are just stories and that neither the king nor his city ever existed. Many historians today say that although there may have been a real person, whom we know as King Arthur, there was no such place as Camelot.

We cannot investigate all these ideas in this inquiry. All we can do is to look at one place that may have been Camelot. You may like to investigate further for yourselves.

## Reading stories and legends
In May 1959 the American novelist, John Steinbeck, wrote home to his friends:

> Somerset 1st May 1959
>
> To Eve and Chase
>
> Yesterday, something wonderful. It was a golden day and the apple blossoms are out and for the first time I climbed to Cadbury—Camelot. . . . Could see from the Bristol Channel to the top of the Mendips and all the little villages. Glastonbury Tor . . . on the other side. I shall come back over and over, but what a day to see it first.

(John Steinbeck, *The Acts of King Arthur and his Noble Knights*)

Camelot and the stories of King Arthur were important to John Steinbeck because they had changed his life. When he was a boy he disliked reading. He says, 'I remember that words—written or printed—were devils and books, because they gave me pain, were my enemies.'

Then one of his aunts gave him a copy of *The Morte D'Arthur* ('The death of Arthur'). This book is a collection of stories about King Arthur and his knights and was written by Sir Thomas Malory in the fifteenth century. The ancient words and strange names in it were hard to read and understand.

The young Steinbeck 'stared at the black print with hatred, then gradually the pages opened,' he writes, 'and let me in.'

As he read on, the people of King Arthur's court became as real to him as the people of his own home town. A man who was usually honest might use tricks to get something he wanted badly. Men and women fell in and out of love.

People who should have been trustworthy were really deceitful and evil.

Steinbeck was entranced by this world that was so strange and yet familiar. Through the stories he learned to love reading and went on to become a famous writer. He believed, as do many historians, that the stories about King Arthur are a mixture of fact and fiction. Once, he thought, there lived a great warrior who defended his people against their enemies. This king gained a reputation for courage and leadership. Even after his death, people were influenced by his example and told and retold stories about him. As time went on, their memories of what really happened faded, but they went on adding legends to the facts of history.

John Steinbeck had come to the English countryside because he wanted to write these stories of Arthur yet again. He wanted to tell them in 'plain, present-day speech for people living today'. To do this well, he wanted to see for himself the places connected with the stories. That was why he had climbed South Cadbury Hill on that 'golden day'.

He believed that if there was a real King Arthur there must have been a real Camelot. It might have been different from the turreted city that Sir Thomas Malory described, but it had existed. John Steinbeck thought that its ruins lay under South Cadbury hilltop. When he looked out over the Somerset countryside he was convinced he was looking at Arthur's kingdom.

## Your work
1 Think of a book or film on a historical subject that has made you want to visit a place connected with it. What buildings and remains connected with your story would you look for? Explain why.
2 What did John Steinbeck mean when he said it had been a 'golden day'? (Was it just the weather?) He said he would go back 'over and over'. How would this help him to write his book? Give an example of how a visit to a place of interest has helped you to understand its history better.
3 Think of a book or film you know about people who lived in a different place or time, but who seem real to you.

(a) In which ways was their way of life different from yours? (What were their homes like? How did they travel?)

(b) In which ways were the problems that people faced similar to ours today? (Did they have to cope with rapid change? Did they have to find new ways of earning a living?)

(c) How did their character and behaviour remind you of yourself and people you know?

## What do you think?

John Steinbeck believed that South Cadbury was Camelot, but he could not prove it.

Why should a historian always tell you if he believes something but cannot prove it?

## Talking about the past: oral tradition

Before most people could read or write they relied on their memories for a record of what happened in the past. Men and women passed on the stories they had heard from their parents by telling them to their children. In this way they built up what we call an 'oral tradition'. When stories are retold for centuries, they are bound to be altered in some way, but usually they still keep some of the original truth. Today, some historians believe we should pay attention to these oral traditions. They may give us the clues to the past that we are looking for.

In Somerset, each new generation of people has handed down stories about King Arthur for hundreds of years. It is claimed that the hill at South Cadbury was where King Arthur held his court, though no one remembers *why* people believe this. When John Leland, who lived in the reign of Henry VII, visited this area in 1542, he wrote:

> At South Cadburi standith Camallate, sumtyme a famose toun or castle. The people can tell nothing thar but they have hard say that Arture much resortid to Camallate.

To this day, the flat area on the crest of the hill is known as 'King Arthur's Palace'. At the foot of the hill, a spring gushes out of the ground. It is said that if you go there on St John's Eve at Midsummer, you will hear hoof-beats, though you will not see anything. The spirits of Arthur and his knights are riding to the spring to drink and give water to their ghostly horses.

From the top of South Cadbury you can see Glastonbury Tor and its ancient abbey. In the thirteenth century a Welsh minstrel told King Henry II that Arthur's body was buried in the abbey grounds. Henry ordered the monks to dig in the place that the minstrel had described. Another Welshman, Gerald of Wales, a historian who lived at that time, later reported what happened. We can usually rely on his information.

Buried deep in the earth, he writes, the monks found a stone slab. Beneath this was a cross made of lead. On it was inscribed,

HIC IACET SEPULTUS INCLYTUS REX ARTHURUS CUM WENNEVARIA UXORE SECUNDA IN INSULA AVALONIA

▲ William Camden's drawing of the cross he found at Glastonbury. The Latin words read: HIC IACET SEPULTUS INCLITUS REX ARTURIUS IN INSULA AVALONIA

This means: 'Here lies buried the famous King Arthur with Guinevere, his second wife, in the Isle of Avalon'. (This part of Somerset is known as 'the Isle of Avalon'.)

As the monks dug deeper, their spades struck a wooden coffin. It was made from the hollowed-out trunk of an oak tree. Inside were the skeletons of a man and woman. The man's skull was scarred with wounds that had healed over. These showed that he had been wounded in the head at least ten times during his life, but had survived. One large hole showed where he had been struck and fatally wounded. This wound had not healed. Around the woman's skull lay a tress of yellow hair. One of the monks could not resist touching it. At once, it crumbled into dust.

Three hundred years later, William Camden visited Glastonbury. He found a cross, with Arthur's name carved on it, still standing in the grounds of the abbey. Camden, who was writing a book about the old buildings of Britain and their histories, made a drawing of the cross. This drawing and the account we have by Gerald of Wales are all we have left to show that the grave ever existed.

## Your work

1 *Repeating a story*

Divide the class into lines going from the front to the back of the room. The teacher calls the first person in each row together and tells them a short story. The rest of the class must not hear.

The first person in each row now repeats the story to the person behind and so on. The last person in each row repeats what he or she was told to the whole class.

(a) In what ways has the story been altered?

(b) Does this tell us anything about the reliability of oral traditions?

2 What legends do you know about places in your neighbourhood? Could any part of the legend be true? Give reasons for your answer.

3 Compare the words on the cross as recorded by Gerald of Wales with those on the cross drawn by William Camden.

(a) What do you notice?

(b) Does this strengthen or weaken your belief that the grave ever existed? Give reasons for your answer.

## What do you think?

Oral tradition alone is not enough to prove that something happened or existed. We need other kinds of evidence as well, for example written records or remains of buildings. What other kinds of evidence might we look for to help us prove that South Cadbury was Camelot?

## Making a historical reconstruction

Although there are many legends about King Arthur, ancient history books tell us very little about him. Some modern historians believe that Arthur never existed. Others have searched for all the clues they can find to show that he was a real person.

Look at the time chart. It shows you when they think he lived, and when they think his city of Camelot was built. (The letter *c* in front of a date means 'about'.)

In legends the exact date when something happened does not matter, but a real event must have happened at a particular time. This is why we need to know the date when we think Camelot was built. Without this information, we would not know the kind of ruins we were looking for.

| Date | Events |
|---|---|
| 410 | The Roman army left Britain. The Britons organised their own armies to defend themselves against foreign invaders. |
| c 425 | Anglo-Saxon raiders from Germany attacked Britain, Vortigern, a British leader, paid some Anglo-Saxons to fight in his army against the invaders. |
| 450 | The Anglo-Saxon troops defending Britain rebelled. They seized land in the east of Britain. |
| c 500 | The Battle of Mount Badon. The Britons defeated the Anglo-Saxons and checked their advance. There was a period of peace. |
| c 542 | The Battle of Camlann (Camelot). Arthur is said to have been defeated in battle, possibly fighting against other Britons. He died of his wounds. |

**Your work**

Historians who believe that there was a real Arthur think he was a Briton. If they are right:

1 Which people would he have been fighting against?
2 For about how many years was he in power?
3 In which century did he rule?
4 Between which two dates on the time chart was Camelot built? Give reasons for your answer.

**What do you think?**

Consider what you have learnt so far about South Cadbury. Is there any proof that a city stood there in the century when Arthur was alive? Give reasons for your answer.

**Studying the landscape**

Everything changes with time. The Somerset countryside has slowly altered over the centuries. If Camelot stood on South Cadbury, the view its people saw from their hilltop was different in some ways from the scene today.

As now, the high points of Glastonbury Tor and the Mendips stood out against the skyline. On a clear day, the waters of the Bristol Channel were visible. But instead of little villages, miles and miles of lonely marshland stretched between the Mendips and the Quantocks. This area was often flooded, so people built their homes on higher ground. Travellers who knew the area well might risk going on foot through the marshes. Most people, however, felt safer making their way in small boats along the streams that fed the Avon and the Parrett.

To the west, on firmer ground, ran the Fosse Way. The stones of this old Roman road were cracked and uneven, but it could still be used. Older paths, called ridgeways, ran along the crests of the hills. Modern archaeologists have studied this landscape carefully. Their discoveries show us how men who lived long ago used its hills and rivers to defend themselves from attack.

**Your work**

*South Cadbury Hill*

1 Look at the photograph. Why would the hill itself have been a good place to build a stronghold?

▲ South Cadbury today from the air, looking from the east

134

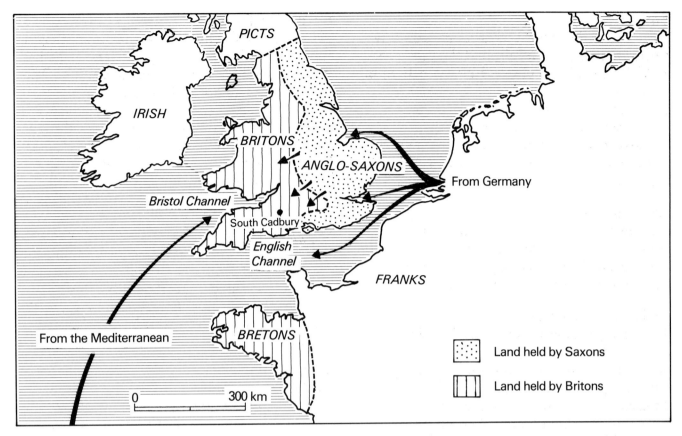

▲ The frontier between the natives and the invaders in about 500

2 Look at the maps on this page. If the Anglo-Saxons attacked by land, from which direction would they have come? Was South Cadbury in a good position to check an attack on South West Britain?
(Consider hills, rivers and the coastline as checks to an invader.)

3 Which routeways would the defenders of South Cadbury have used
(a) to bring in supplies from Britain and abroad?
(b) to launch an attack on the Anglo-Saxons?

*Other strong points*
Using the key to the map on the right find Wansdyke. This ditch is nearly 80 km long. It was built in the sixth century to stop an attack from the north. Find the three strongholds. These hill-forts were rebuilt by chieftains who lived in the sixth century. From Brent Knoll you can see both Dinas Powys and Glastonbury. From Glastonbury you can see South Cadbury.

1 It must have taken much time and effort to make Wansdyke and rebuild the hill forts.

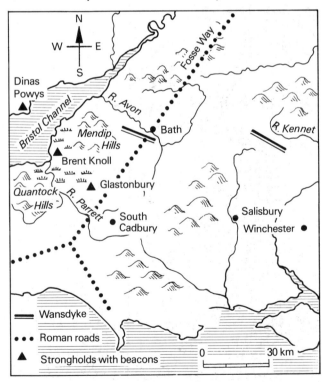

▼ The country around South Cadbury

Why did the people of the time make this effort?

2 What might the hilltop forts have been used for, as well as strongholds?

**3** Which waterways would Dinas Powys and Brent Knoll have guarded? Why might Wansdyke have been built to the south of the Avon and the Kennet? Why was it important to the Britons to control these waterways?

## Summing up

**1** Which of these statements do you find most convincing? Give reasons for your answer.
In the sixth century, chieftains in south-west Britain
(a) certainly co-operated to defend themselves against the Anglo-Saxons.
(b) probably co-operated to defend themselves against the Anglo-Saxons.
(c) may have co-operated to defend themselves against the Anglo-Saxons.
**2** Would South Cadbury have been a good place to build a stronghold? Give reasons for your answer.

## What do you think?

Archaeological excavations are expensive. Consider everything you have learnt about South Cadbury so far. Would it be worth excavating South Cadbury to see if a town or fortress ever stood there? Give reasons for your answer.

## Carrying out an archaeological excavation

Near South Cadbury lived Mrs Mary Hartfield, who was interested in archaeology. In the 1950s she often climbed to the summit of the hill to search for **shards,** or fragments of pottery. Mrs Hartfield looked carefully among the stones and grass on the hilltop. Whenever she added a shard to her collection she made a note of exactly where she found it. She gave her collection to the Somerset County Museum at Taunton, where it was examined by Dr Ralegh Radford, an archaeologist. Some of the fragments were a reddish-brown colour. Looking at these pieces under a microscope, Dr Radford could see that they came from a type of pot called Tintagel ware. The illustration shows you what this kind of pottery was like.

Dr Radford had wanted to excavate South Cadbury for a long time. Like the local people, he knew that part of the summit was called 'King Arthur's Palace'. Now that the shards of Tintagel ware had been found, he knew that it was worth spending money on excavation.

If you study the illustrations and answer the questions, you will see why.

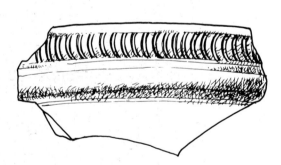

▲ A shard of reddish-brown Tintagel ware, dating from the sixth century. The shard was once part of a jar. Notice the rim and ridges of the shard. A rope was passed under the rim and along the line of the ridges so that the jar could be carried safely

▶ An **amphora** or storage jar. Amphorae like this one were made in the eastern Mediterranean region and used to store or transport wine and oil

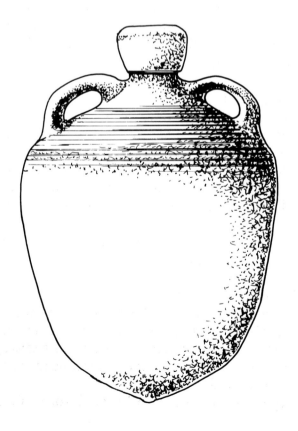

**The amphorae and the date when Camelot was built**

1 What did people use the amphorae for?
2 In which century do people seem to have been using amphorae at South Cadbury?
3 When do we think that Camelot was built?
4 Were people using amphorae on South Cadbury when Camelot would have stood there?

**The goods in the amphorae and the leader who imported them**

1 Where did the oil and wine in the amphorae come from?
2 Why would they have been expensive for people living in Britain?
3 What does this show us about the wealth of the leader at South Cadbury?
4 Is it possible that Arthur was the leader at South Cadbury? Give reasons for your answer.

**Digging up the stronghold**

From 1966 to 1970 a team of archaeologists excavated South Cadbury. They could not dig up all the vast summit, so they surveyed the ground carefully before they began.

By using modern equipment they could tell which areas of soil had been disturbed in the past. They were most likely to find the remains of buildings in these areas. The illustrations show you how the archaeologists did this and what they found.

**King Arthur's Palace**

The large circle was once a ditch. The large dark holes are storage pits. These were made in the Iron Age, by the people who lived in Britain before the Romans came and who built the first stronghold at Cadbury. There are also some holes in straight lines. These may have been the post holes, where the upright timbers for a large wooden hall stood. This could have dated from King Arthur's time.

**Walls, gates and towers**

Dr Alcock, the archaeologist in charge, and his helpers also dug into the ramparts and examined the foundations of an old gateway. From what they found, they were able to reconstruct the following events.

In the sixth century, a British leader and his people came to South Cadbury. They found the stone and earth ramparts of the old Iron Age camp. They rebuilt the stone ramparts, driving upright timbers into the stones to form a wooden wall. At intervals, rising above the wall, they made look-out towers.

The gateway was strong and could not easily be passed. Above the entrance there was probably a look-out tower, where a sentry challenged all comers. An enemy would have to break down the great double doors, each about 1.5 m across. These met in the middle of the entrance and were barred on the inside. Even then an attacker would find two inner doors facing him which he would also have to batter down.

▲ The 'banjo' is an instrument that detects places where the soil has been disturbed. These places are plotted on a chart

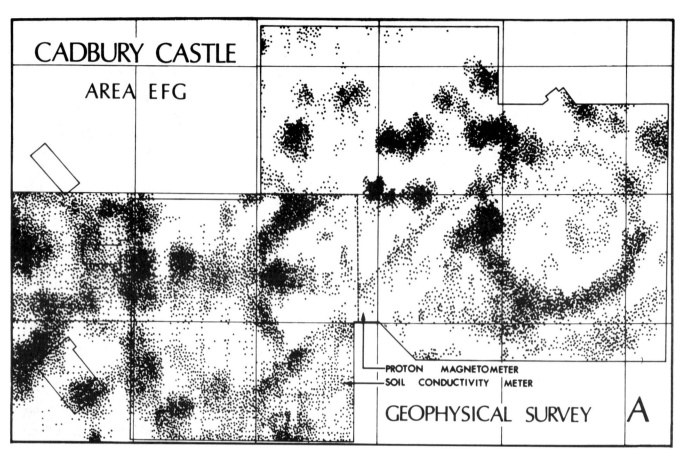

CADBURY CASTLE

AREA EFG

PROTON MAGNETOMETER
SOIL CONDUCTIVITY METER

GEOPHYSICAL SURVEY

A

▲ A dot density chart. The dots show places where buildings may have stood

▼ The area shown on the dot density chart has been excavated to show the remains of a settlement

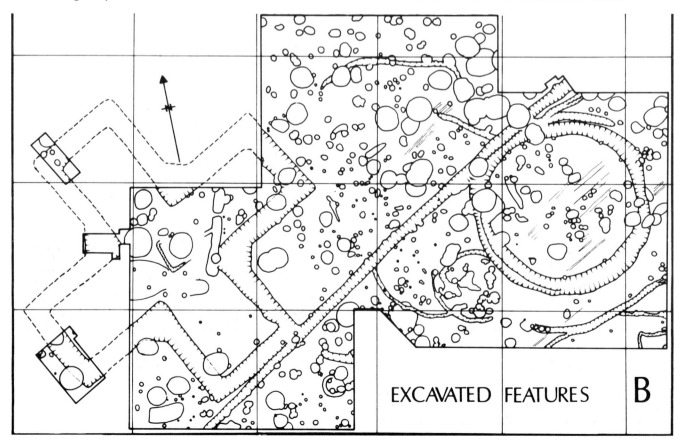

EXCAVATED FEATURES

B

▼ The white pegs stand in the holes that once held the upright timbers of a wooden hall

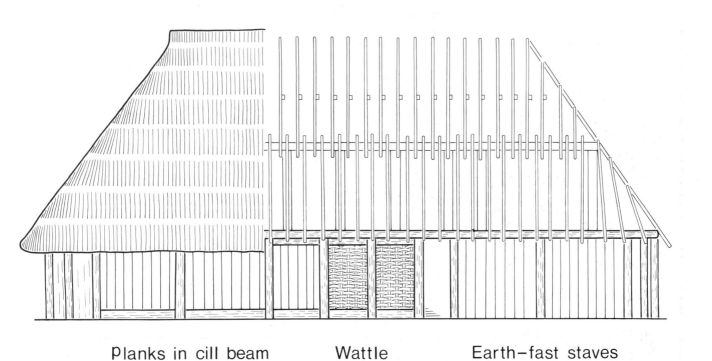

Planks in cill beam    Wattle    Earth–fast staves

▲ Judging from the size and position of the post holes, the hall would have looked like this. The hall was large, and was probably built for an important leader and his followers

▼ The wall, watch tower and gateway probably looked like this

## Summing up

1 The stories about King Arthur and Camelot may be based on fact or they may be pure fiction. There may have been a real Arthur but not a real Camelot.

2 Several places in Britain, from Edinburgh to Cornwall, may have been Camelot. We have looked at one place only, South Cadbury in Somerset.

3 The fortress at South Cadbury was built at about the time when Arthur, if he was a real person, would have lived.

## What do you think?

If there was a real Arthur, which of these statements do you think is the most accurate?

> South Cadbury was Camelot.
> South Cadbury was probably Camelot.
> South Cadbury may have been Camelot.
> South Cadbury has nothing to do with Camelot.

Give reasons for your answer.

▲ The sixth-century British warrior may have looked like this—there isn't enough evidence for us to be certain

## Books about Camelot and King Arthur

*Stories based on the legends about King Arthur*

Marigold, D., *Lancelot and Elaine: A Lost Love* (John Murray 1983)

Reyersbach, A., *The Grail Quest: From Frost to Flower* (John Murray 1983)

Steinbeck, J., *The Acts of King Arthur and his Noble Knights based on the Winchester Manuscript of Sir Thomas Malory* (Heinemann 1976)

Sutcliff, R., *The Sword and the Circle* (Bodley Head 1981)

White, T. H., *The Once and Future King* (Collins 1938)

White, T. H., *The Sword in the Stone* (Collins 1959)

*Historical background*

Crossley-Holland, K., *Green Blades Rising* (André Deutsch 1975)

*Background books for teachers*

Ashe, G., *All About King Arthur* (W. H. Allen 1969)

Ashe, G., *Camelot and the Vision of Albion* (Panther 1975)

# 7 Topic Work

You know by now that good historians:
    gather information carefully,
    quote information accurately,
    study information to find answers to questions,
    use information to form their own opinions.
Writing about a topic gives you a chance to show *your* skill at writing history.

---

### Subjects for topic work

You will find information in this book on:

Homes and Furniture
Farming and Food
Kings and Government
Warriors and Warfare
Towns and Townspeople
Monks and Monasteries

Do not choose your topic yet.

---

## Finding your information
1 *Pictures, plans and maps*
(In pairs)
(a) Look at the picture on page 61. Which topic does this picture illustrate?
(b) Look through the illustrations in this book and find a picture, plan or map to illustrate each of the other topics.
2 *Writing*
(In pairs)
(a) Look up 'T' in the *Index*, find Towns, and turn to the first page number after this word. Does it tell you about Roman, Saxon, or Norman towns?
(b) Which subjects for topics would you look up under the letters 'K' and 'M'? Turn to one or two page numbers and see what they tell you about these subjects.

## Choosing a topic
1 Choose a topic from the list given above.
2 Draw two or three pictures, plans or maps to illustrate your topic. Write one or two sentences about each illustration.

3 Using the *Index*, choose *four* interesting pieces of information about your topic *from at least three sections* of this book. For example, if you choose 'Warriors and Warfare', you might write about: a Roman soldier, a Viking warrior, a Norman knight.
4 Copy each piece of information accurately, and give the number of the page where you found it. For example:

---

'The kings and their chieftains all had bands of fighting men equipped with swords, shields and axes. ... They were well trained, and the Viking warrior with his pointed helmet, thick leather tunic and battle-axe was feared and respected all over Europe.' (page 78)

---

Why is the extract written in inverted commas?
What does the row of dots show?
5 Use books from the History section of your school library to find out more about your topic. Look at the Contents lists and Indexes of books, as well as their titles.
6 Write a conclusion to your topic, saying why you chose this subject, and which piece of information you found the most interesting or surprising.

## Sharing your information
When you have all finished your topics, you may like to share your findings in one of the following ways.
1 *Make a 'Did You Know?' sheet.*
(a) Divide your class into four groups
(b) In each group, pass round a large sheet of paper on which everyone writes *one* interesting piece of information from his or her topic.
(c) Display your sheets when they are completed.
2 *Make a book.*
In groups of three, put topics on three different subjects together to form three chapters in a book. Make a front cover, with a title for your book. Draw a picture on the back cover, make a contents page.

Pass your books around for other people to read.

**3** *Form a reviewing panel.*

In groups of three, review the topics of the two other people in your group.

(a) Illustrations:
Do they help us to understand the subject more clearly?

(b) Writing:
Is the information interesting?
Can we check that it is accurate?
Is it accurate?

(c) In your opinion, is it:
a fairly good piece of work?
a good piece of work?
an excellent piece of work?

Give reasons for your answer.

# Summing up

### Time chart
Make a time chart to cover the years AD 11 to AD 1200.

Begin your chart as shown below:

| Century AD | Year | Important event | Illustration |
|---|---|---|---|
| 1 | 43 | The Romans invade Britain | |

**1** Choose two important events from each century and enter them on your chart.

**2** Does your chart cover more or less than a millennium?

**3** Which is the longer period of time, from the Roman invasion to the death of Henry II or from Henry's death to today?

### Making a map of our ancestors' settlements
Most people living in Britain today are descended from a mixture of all the invaders who settled in these islands. More descendants of these settlers are to be found in some parts of Britain than in others.

**1** Draw an outline map of Great Britain and label England, Ireland, Scotland and Wales.

**2** Many people who live in Scotland, Wales and Ireland are descended from the Celts or British tribes who lived in Britain before the Romans came. Write Celts in these three countries on your map.

**3** Complete your map by writing Saxons, Norwegians, Danes or Normans in areas where you think that these invaders would have settled in large numbers.

### Find the deliberate mistakes
The sentence which follows might appear in a piece of topic work. It contains one deliberate mistake. See if you can find it.

Above the kitchen, and connected to it by a spiral staircase, was the hall. This was the biggest room in the cathedral. (pp. 93–4)

### How do we know?
We know about the death of Bede from reading Cuthwin's letter to Cuthbert. How do we know about the following?

Boudica's rebellion
The Battle of Hastings
The murder of Thomas Becket

### What do you think?
**1** Would a Norman baron living in Shrewsbury in 1100 have understood the language of a Welsh peasant?

**2** Did all the people in Britain in the reign of Henry II feel that they belonged to the same nation?

**3** Did the Pope's influence in England increase or decrease after the murder of Thomas Becket in Canterbury cathedral? Give reasons for your answer.

### Who or which came first?
**1** The people listed below had all settled in Britain by the end of the period that you have studied. List them in the correct chronological order:

Normans    Romans    Vikings
Saxons    Britons    Danes

**2** These buildings were built in Britain in the period that you have studied. List them in the correct chronological order:

motte and bailey castle    villa
king's great hall    stone keep

**3** Make up your own 'Who or which came first?' quiz.

# Glossary

| | |
|---|---|
| **acre** | an area of land: 0.404 hectares |
| **amphitheatre** | circular theatre used by the Romans for all kinds of entertainments |
| **amphora (pl. amphorae)** | two-handled jar for holding wine or oil |
| **Anglo-Saxons** | the invaders from northern Germany and southern Denmark who occupied part of Britain after the Romans left |
| **arable land** | ploughed farmland |
| **bailey** | courtyard of a Norman castle |
| **ballista** | stone-throwing machine used by the Romans |
| **basilica** | grand building used for meetings of townspeople |
| **Britannia** | Roman province made up of present-day England and Wales |
| **Britain** | England, Wales and Scotland |
| **burgh** | small walled town |
| **-by** | Danish place-name ending, meaning village or homestead |
| **Celts** | first inhabitants of Britain and western Europe |
| **chain mail** | flexible armour made from small interlocking metal rings |
| **distaff** | the stick from which the wool is pulled in spinning |
| **England** | the part of Britain where the Anglo-Saxons settled |
| **excavate** | dig up |
| **forum** | large open-air meeting place where people came together |
| **fuller** | person who whitened cloth after it was woven |
| **galley** | boat rowed by slaves |
| **Gaul** | present-day France |
| **javelin** | light spear that was thrown |

| | |
|---|---|
| keep | the strongest and safest part of a castle |
| mead | alcoholic drink made with fermented honey |
| moot | meeting of free men |
| mosaic | tiny tiles arranged to form a pattern on floors |
| motte | mound on which Norman keeps were built |
| palisade | strong wooden fence |
| parchment | document made of treated animal skin |
| podium | stone foundation or base |
| quill | stiff feather used for writing |
| rampart | earth wall |
| reeve | foreman on a manor |
| shard | broken piece of pottery |
| shilling | 12 (old) pence |
| soapstone | soft stone used to make cooking pots and dishes |
| standard | a pole with metal badges fixed to it, sometimes topped by a bronze eagle |
| stockade | a wall made of wooden stakes |
| synod | official meeting of church leaders |
| tanner | person who soaked hides to soften them and turn them into leather |
| thane | Saxon nobleman |
| thorpe | Danish word meaning a small village |
| toft | Danish word meaning a house |
| -ton | Anglo-Saxon place-name ending meaning a homestead |
| tribute | tax or protection money paid to an overlord |
| verify | find out the truth |
| vicus | small village |
| Vikings | the inhabitants of Norway, Sweden and Denmark |

| villa | Roman farm |
| --- | --- |
| yoke | wooden bar used for joining two animals together to pull heavy loads |

# Index

The subjects for topic work mentioned on page 142
are printed in **BOLD CAPITALS**.

Page numbers in **bold** refer to illustrations.